Python Requests Essentials

Learn how to integrate your applications seamlessly
with web services using Python Requests

Rakesh Vidya Chandra

Bala Subrahmanyam Varanasi

[PACKT] open source*
PUBLISHING   community experience distilled

BIRMINGHAM - MUMBAI

Python Requests Essentials

Copyright © 2015 Packt Publishing

First published: June 2015

Production reference: 1120615

Published by Packt Publishing Ltd.
Livery Place
35 Livery Street
Birmingham B3 2PB, UK.

ISBN 978-1-78439-541-4

www.packtpub.com

Credits

About the Authors

Rakesh Vidya Chandra has been in the field of software development for the last 3 years. His love for programming first sparked when he was introduced to LOGO in his school. After obtaining his bachelor's degree in Information Technology, he worked with Agiliq Info Solutions and built several web applications using Python. Rakesh is passionate about writing technical blogs on various open source technologies. When not coding, he loves to dance to hip-hop and listens to EDM.

Bala Subrahmanyam Varanasi loves hacking and building web applications. He has a bachelor's degree in Information Technology. He has been in the software industry for the last three and a half years, where he worked with Agiliq Info Solutions and Crypsis Technologies. Bala has also built different web applications using Python, Ruby, and JavaScript. Apart from coding, he is interested in entrepreneurship and is the founder of Firebolt Labs. Currently, he is working as a software engineer at TinyOwl Technology.

Acknowledgments

We are indebted to Kenneth Rietz for building a beautiful Python library, which helped the Python world interact with the Web seamlessly. We especially wish to thank Thejaswi Puthraya, Javed Khan, and Daniel Roy Greenfeld for guiding us and encouraging us on this journey.

Our content editors, Ritika Singh and Reshma Raman, have helped us all the way, and at this juncture, we would like to thank them wholeheartedly. We would especially like to thank Packt Publishing; our technical reviewers, Islu Park, Yves Dorfsman, and Kirk Strauser; and our technical editor, Shivani Mistry, for their valuable ideas and suggestions.

We express our heartfelt gratitude to our college chairman, Mr. K.V.Vishnu Raju, who stood as an inspiration to us. We would like to thank our college principal, Dr. D. Suryanaryana, for helping us be enthusiastic. It's our duty to express our thanks to our alma mater, Vishnu Institute of Technology, for being the matrix of our education.

We are grateful to our teachers Dr. Ramadevi, Mrs. M. Sri Lakshmi, and Mr. Krishna Chaitanya Varma Alluri for motivating us all the way.

Finally, we would like to acknowledge with gratitude, the support and love from all of our family members, friends, and well wishers.

About the Reviewers

Yves Dorfsman is a system administrator and a developer with experience in oil and gas, financial, and software industries. He has extensive experience in Python, both in sysadmin tasks and automation, and in software development.

Ilsu Park is an entrepreneur and software engineer currently living in Seoul, South Korea. He studied computer science from KAIST and was a member of the hacking and security group in college. He has a research experience in RFID security, and his interests are decentralized networks, concurrency handling, and highly scalable architecture. He also has contributed to various open source projects, including Python requests and the tornado web server. He is most passionate about building a great company.

Kirk Strauser is a software architect from San Francisco Bay Area and has used Python personally and professionally for over 15 years. He loves learning new things, and mentors a Curiosity Hacked guild to share his experiences with the next generation of programmers and hackers.

> I'd like to thank my lovely wife, Jennifer, and the rest of my family for their patience with my projects.

www.PacktPub.com

Support files, eBooks, discount offers, and more

For support files and downloads related to your book, please visit www.PacktPub.com.

Did you know that Packt offers eBook versions of every book published, with PDF and ePub files available? You can upgrade to the eBook version at www.PacktPub.com and as a print book customer, you are entitled to a discount on the eBook copy. Get in touch with us at service@packtpub.com for more details.

At www.PacktPub.com, you can also read a collection of free technical articles, sign up for a range of free newsletters and receive exclusive discounts and offers on Packt books and eBooks.

https://www2.packtpub.com/books/subscription/packtlib

Do you need instant solutions to your IT questions? PacktLib is Packt's online digital book library. Here, you can search, access, and read Packt's entire library of books.

Why subscribe?

- Fully searchable across every book published by Packt
- Copy and paste, print, and bookmark content
- On demand and accessible via a web browser

Free access for Packt account holders

If you have an account with Packt at www.PacktPub.com, you can use this to access PacktLib today and view 9 entirely free books. Simply use your login credentials for immediate access.

Table of Contents

Preface

Python is one of the evolving language of our era, and it's gaining a lot of attention these days. It is one of the powerful and flexible open source languages instilled with powerful libraries. For every python developer, Requests is the library that comes to mind first when he/she needs to interact with the Web. With its batteries included Requests turned the process of interacting with Web a cakewalk and stands as one of the world's best client with more than 42 million downloads.

With the rise of social media, APIs turn to be a must have part of every application, and interacting with them in the best way possible is going to be a challenge. Getting to know how to interact with APIs, building an API, scraping the web, and such stuff will help every budding web developer to reach new heights.

What this book covers

Chapter 1, *Interacting with the Web Using Requests*, covers topics such as why Requests is better than urllib2, how to make a simple request, different types of response content, adding custom headers to our Requests, dealing with form encoded data, using the status code lookup, locating the request redirection, location, and timeouts.

Chapter 2, *Digging Deep into Requests*, talks about using session objects. It discusses the structure of request and response, prepared Requests, SSL verification with Requests, streaming uploads, generators, and event hooks. This chapter also demonstrates using proxies, link headers, and transport headers.

Chapter 3, *Authenticating with Requests*, introduces you to the different types of procedures that are in practice for authentication. You will gain knowledge on authenticating with OAuth1, digest authentication, and basic authentication.

Chapter 4, Mocking HTTP Requests Using HTTPretty, covers HTTPretty along with its installation and usage. Then, we deal with real-time examples and learn how to mimic the actions of a server using Python Requests and HTTPretty.

Chapter 5, Interacting with Social Media Using Requests, covers significant ground. Starting with an introduction to the Twitter API, Facebook API, and reddit API, we will move on to discover ways in which we can obtain keys, create an authentication request, and work with various examples to interact with social media.

Chapter 6, Web Scraping with Python Requests and BeautifulSoup, empowers you to have a better understanding of the libraries that are used in scraping the Web. You will also be introduced to using the BeautifulSoup library, its installation, and procedures to scrape the web using Python Requests and BeautifulSoup.

 We would like to thank www.majortests.com for allowing us to base the examples in this chapter around their website.

Chapter 7, Implementing a Web Application with Python Using Flask, gives an introduction to the Flask framework and moves on to discuss how to develop a simple Survey application which deals with creating, listing and voting various questions. In this chapter you will acquire all the knowledge required to build a web application using Flask.

What you need for this book

You need the following software for this book:

- Python 2.7 or above
- Python Requests
- BeautifulSoup
- HTTPretty
- Flask

Who this book is for

This book is for all Python developers, web developers, and even administrators who want to use Requests to make HTTP Requests to web servers and perform HTML scraping.

Conventions

In this book, you will find a number of text styles that distinguish between different kinds of information. Here are some examples of these styles and an explanation of their meaning.

Code words in text, database table names, folder names, filenames, file extensions, pathnames, dummy URLs, user input, and Twitter handles are shown as follows: "The process includes importing the `Requests` module, and then getting the web page with `get` method."

A block of code is set as follows:

```
parameters = {'key1': 'value1', 'key2': 'value2'}
r = requests.get('url', params=parameters)
```

Any command-line input or output is written as follows:

```
>>> r = requests.get('http://google.com')
```

New terms and **important words** are shown in bold. Words that you see on the screen, for example, in menus or dialog boxes, appear in the text like this: "Click on **Create New App** button."

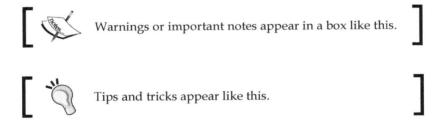

Warnings or important notes appear in a box like this.

Tips and tricks appear like this.

Reader feedback

Feedback from our readers is always welcome. Let us know what you think about this book—what you liked or disliked. Reader feedback is important for us as it helps us develop titles that you will really get the most out of.

To send us general feedback, simply e-mail feedback@packtpub.com, and mention the book's title in the subject of your message.

If there is a topic that you have expertise in and you are interested in either writing or contributing to a book, see our author guide at www.packtpub.com/authors.

Customer support

Now that you are the proud owner of a Packt book, we have a number of things to help you to get the most from your purchase.

Downloading the example code

You can download the example code files from your account at http://www.packtpub.com for all the Packt Publishing books you have purchased. If you purchased this book elsewhere, you can visit http://www.packtpub.com/support and register to have the files e-mailed directly to you.

Errata

Although we have taken every care to ensure the accuracy of our content, mistakes do happen. If you find a mistake in one of our books—maybe a mistake in the text or the code—we would be grateful if you could report this to us. By doing so, you can save other readers from frustration and help us improve subsequent versions of this book. If you find any errata, please report them by visiting http://www.packtpub.com/submit-errata, selecting your book, clicking on the **Errata Submission Form** link, and entering the details of your errata. Once your errata are verified, your submission will be accepted and the errata will be uploaded to our website or added to any list of existing errata under the Errata section of that title.

To view the previously submitted errata, go to https://www.packtpub.com/books/content/support and enter the name of the book in the search field. The required information will appear under the **Errata** section.

Piracy

Piracy of copyrighted material on the Internet is an ongoing problem across all media. At Packt, we take the protection of our copyright and licenses very seriously. If you come across any illegal copies of our works in any form on the Internet, please provide us with the location address or website name immediately so that we can pursue a remedy.

Please contact us at copyright@packtpub.com with a link to the suspected pirated material.

We appreciate your help in protecting our authors and our ability to bring you valuable content.

Questions

If you have a problem with any aspect of this book, you can contact us at questions@packtpub.com, and we will do our best to address the problem.

1
Interacting with the Web Using Requests

Reading data and obtaining information from web services tends to be a crucial task in these modern days. Everyone knows how an **Application Programming Interface (API)** allowed Facebook to spread the use of the Like button all over the Web and dominated the field of social communication. It has got its own flair to influence the business development, product development and supply chain management. At this stage, learning an efficient way to deal with the API's and opening the web URLs is the need of the hour. This will greatly affect many processes of web development.

Introduction to HTTP request

Whenever our Web browser tries communicating with a Web server, it is done by using the **Hypertext Transfer Protocol (HTTP)** which functions as a request-response protocol. In this process of communication, we send a request to the web server and expect a response in return. Take an example of downloading a PDF from a website. We send a request saying "Get me this specific file", and we get a response from the Web server with "Here is the file followed by the file itself". The HTTP request we are sending possibly has much interesting information. Let us dig inside it.

Here is the raw information of the HTTP request, that I have sent through my device. We can grasp the important parts of the request after looking at the following example:

```
* Connected to google.com (74.125.236.35) port 80 (#0)
> GET / HTTP/1.1
> User-Agent: curl/7.35.0
> Host: google.com
> Accept: */*
>
< HTTP/1.1 302 Found
```

```
< Cache-Control: private
< Content-Type: text/html; charset=UTF-8
< Location: http://www.google.co.in/?gfe_rd=cr&ei=_
qMUVKLCIa3M8gewuoCYBQ
< Content-Length: 261
< Date: Sat, 13 Sep 2014 20:07:26 GMT
* Server GFE/2.0 is not blacklisted
< Server: GFE/2.0
< Alternate-Protocol: 80:quic,p=0.002
```

Now, we will send a request to the server. Let us make use of these parts of the HTTP request:

- **Method**: The GET / http /1.1 in the preceding example, is the HTTP method which is case sensitive. Here are some of the HTTP request methods:
    - ° GET: This fetches information from the given server using the given URI.
    - ° HEAD: The functionality of this is similar to GET but the difference is, it delivers only the status line and header section.
    - ° POST: This can submit data to the server that we wish to process.
    - ° PUT: This creates or overwrites all the current representations of the target resource, when we intend to create a new URL.
    - ° DELETE: This removes all the resources that are described by the given Request-URI.
    - ° OPTIONS: This specifies the communication options for a request/response cycle. It lets the client to mention different options associated with the resource.

- **Request URI**: Uniform Resource Identifier (URI) has the ability to recognize the name of the resource. In the previous example, the hostname is the Request-URI.

- **Request Header fields**: If we want to add more information about the request, we can use the requests header fields. They are colon-separated key value pairs. Some of the request-headers values are:
    - ° Accept-Charset: This is used to indicate the character sets that are acceptable for the response.
    - ° Authorization: This contains the value of the credentials which has the authentication information of the user agent.

- ° `Host`: This identifies the Internet host and port number of the resource that has been requested, using the original URI given by the user.

- ° `User-agent`: It accommodates information about the user agent that originates the request. This can be used for statistical purposes such as tracing the protocol violations.

Python modules

There are some extensively used Python modules which help in opening URLs. Let us have a look at them:

- `httplib2`: This is a comprehensive HTTP client library. It supports many features that are left out of other HTTP libraries. It supports features like caching, keep-alive, compression, redirects and many kinds of authentication.

- `urllib2`: This is an extensively used module for fetching HTTP URLs in a complex world. It defines functions and classes that help with URL actions such as basic and digest authentication, redirections, cookies, and so on.

- `Requests`: This is an Apache2 licensed HTTP library which is written in Python, gifted with many capabilities to result in productivity.

Requests versus urllib2

Let's compare `urllib2` and `Requests`; `urllib2.urlopen()`, which can be used to open a URL (which can be a string or a request object), but there are many other things that can be a burden while interacting with the web. At this point, a simple HTTP library which has the capabilities to make interaction with the web smooth is the need of the hour, and Requests is one of its kind.

The following is an example for fetching the data from a web service with `urllib2` and `Requests` gives us a clear picture of how easy it is to work with `Requests`:

The following code gives an example of `urllib2`:

```
#!/usr/bin/env python
# -*- coding: utf-8 -*-


import urllib2


gh_url = 'https://api.github.com'
```

```
req = urllib2.Request(gh_url)

password_manager = urllib2.HTTPPasswordMgrWithDefaultRealm()
password_manager.add_password(None, gh_url, 'user', 'pass')

auth_manager = urllib2.HTTPBasicAuthHandler(password_manager)
opener = urllib2.build_opener(auth_manager)

urllib2.install_opener(opener)

handler = urllib2.urlopen(req)

print handler.getcode()
print handler.headers.getheader('content-type')

# ------
# 200
# 'application/json'
```

The same example implemented with `Requests`:

```
#!/usr/bin/env python
# -*- coding: utf-8 -*-

import requests

r = requests.get('https://api.github.com', auth=('user', 'pass'))

print r.status_code
print r.headers['content-type']

# ------
# 200
# 'application/json'
```

These examples can be found at https://gist.github.com/kennethreitz/973705.

At this initial stage, the example may look much complicated. Don't go deep into the details of the example. Just see the beauty of requests that allowed us to login to GitHub with very few lines of code. The code with requests seems much simpler and efficient than the urllib2 example. This would help us increase the productivity in all sorts of things.

Essence of Requests

As with HTTP/1.0, HTTP/1.1 has a lot of perks and added features like reusing a connection multiple times which decreases the considerable overhead, keep-alive mechanism, and so on. And fortunately, requests is built from it, giving us the benefits of interacting with the web smoothly and seamlessly. There is no need to manually add query strings to our URLs, or to encode our POST data. Keep-alive and HTTP connection pooling are 100 percent automatic, powered by urllib3, which is embedded within requests. With requests we are gifted with a means to forget about encoding parameters again and again, irrespective of whether it is GET/POST.

There is no requirement for manually adding query strings to the URLs, and also to the features such as connection pooling keep-alive, sessions with cookie persistence, Basic/Digest Authentication, Browser-style SSL Verification, Connection Timeouts, Multipart File Uploads, and so on.

Making a simple request

Now let us create our first request for getting a web page, which is very simple. The process includes importing the requests module, and then getting the web page with the get method. Let us look into an example:

```
>>> import requests
>>> r =  requests.get('http://google.com')
```

Voila! We are done.

In the preceding example, we get the google webpage, using requests.get and saving it in the variable r, which turns out to be the response object. The response object r contains a lot of information about the response, such as header information, content, type of encoding, status code, URL information and many more sophisticated details.

In the same way, we can use all the HTTP request methods like GET, POST, PUT, DELETE, HEAD with requests.

Now let us learn how to pass the parameters in URLs. We can add the parameters to a request using using the params keyword.

The following is the syntax used for passing parameters:

```
parameters = {'key1': 'value1', 'key2': 'value2'}
r = requests.get('url', params=parameters)
```

For getting a clear picture on this, let us get a GitHub user details by logging into GitHub, using requests as shown in the following code:

```
>>> r = requests.get('https://api.github.com/user', auth=('myemailid.mail.com', 'password'))
>>> r.status_code
200
>>> r.url
u'https://api.github.com/user'
>>> r.request
<PreparedRequest [GET]>
```

We have used the auth tuple which enables Basic/Digest/Custom Authentication to login to GitHub and get the user details. The r.status_code result indicates that we have successfully got the user details, and also that we have accessed the URL, and the type of request.

Response content

Response content is the information about the server's response that is delivered back to our console when we send a request.

While interacting with the web, it's necessary to decode the response of the server. While working on an application, there are many cases in which we may have to deal with the raw, or JSON, or even binary response. For this, requests has the capability to automatically decode the content from the server. Requests can smoothly decode many of the Unicode charsets. To add to that, Requests makes informed guesses about the encoding of the response. This basically happens taking the headers into consideration.

If we access the value of r.content, it results us the response content in a raw string format. And if we access r.text, the Requests library encodes the response (r.content value) using r.encoding and returns a new encoding string. In case, if the value of r.encoding is None, Requests assumes the encoding type using r.apparent_encoding, which is provided by the chardet library.

We can access the server's response content in the following way:

```
>>> import requests
>>> r = requests.get('https://google.com')
>>> r.content
'<!doctype html><html itemscope="" itemtype="http://schema.org/WebPage"
.....'
>>> type(r.content)
<type 'str'>
>>> r.text
u'<!doctype html><html itemscope=""\ itemtype="http://schema.org/WebPage"
lang="en-IN"><head><meta content=".......
>>> type(r.text)
<type 'unicode'>
```

In the preceding lines, we try to get the `google` homepage, using `requests.get()` and assigning it to a variable r. The r variable turns out to be a request object here, and we can access the raw content using `r.content` and the encoded response content with `r.text`.

If we wish to find what encoding Requests is using, or if we desire to change the encoding, we can use the property `r.encoding` as shown in the following example:

```
>>> r.encoding
'ISO-8859-1'
>>> r.encoding = 'utf-8'
```

In the first line of the code, we are trying to access the type of encoding that is being followed by Requests. It resulted in `'ISO-8859-1'`. In the next line, I wished to change the encoding to `'utf-8'`. So I assigned the type of encoding to `r.encoding`. If we change the encoding like we did in the second line, Requests tends to use the latest value of `r.encoding` that has been assigned. So from that point in time, it uses the same encoding whenever we call `r.text`.

For an instance, if the value of `r.encoding` is `None`, Requests tend to use the value of `r.apparent_encoding`. The following example explains the case:

```
>>> r.encoding = None
>>> r.apparent_encoding
'ascii'
```

Generally, the value of apparent encoding is specified by the chardet library. With more enthusiasm, if we attempt to set a new encoding type to r.apparent_encoding, Requests raises an AttributeError as its value can't be altered.

```
>>> r.apparent_encoding = 'ISO-8859-1'
Traceback (most recent call last):
  File "<stdin>", line 1, in <module>
AttributeError: can't set attribute
```

Requests are efficient enough to use custom encodings. Take a case in which we have created an encoding of our own, and got it registered with the module of codecs. We can use our custom codec with ease; this is because the values of r.encoding and Requests will take care of the decoding.

Different types of request contents

Requests has the facility to deal with different types of Request contents like binary response content, JSON response content, and raw response content. To give a clear picture on different types of response content, we listed the details. The examples used here are developed using Python 2.7.x.

Custom headers

We can send custom headers with a request. For that, we just need to create a dictionary with our headers and pass the headers parameter in the get, or post method. In the dictionary, key is the name of the header and the value is, well, the value of the pair. Let us pass an HTTP header to a request:

```
>>> import json
>>> url = 'https://api.github.com/some/endpoint'
>>>  payload = {'some': 'data'}
>>> headers = {'Content-Type': 'application/json'}
>>> r = requests.post(url, data=json.dumps(payload), headers=headers)
```

This example has been taken from the Request documents found at `http://docs.python-requests.org/en/latest/user/quickstart/#custom-headers`.

In this example, we have sent a header `content-type` with a value `application/json`, as a parameter to the request.

In the same way, we can send a request with a custom header. Say we have a necessity to send a request with an authorization header with a value as some token. We can create a dictionary with a key `'Authorization'` and value as a token which would look like the following:

```
>>> url = 'some url'
>>> header = {'Authorization' : 'some token'}
>>> r.request.post(url, headers=headers)
```

Sending form-encoded data

We can send form-encoded data like an HTML form using Requests. A simple dictionary to the data argument gets this done. The dictionary of data will turn as form-encoded automatically, when a request is made.

```
>>> payload = {'key1': 'value1', 'key2': 'value2'}
>>> r = request.post("some_url/post", data=payload)
>>> print(r.text)
{
    ...
    "form": {
        "key2": "value2",
      "key1": "value1"
    },
    ...
}
```

In the preceding example, we tried sending data that is form-encoded. While dealing with data that is not form-encoded, we should send a string in the place of a dictionary.

Posting multipart encoded files

We tend to upload multipart data like images or files through POST. We can achieve this in `requests` using `files` which is a dictionary of `'name'` and value of `file-like-objects`. And also we can specify it as `'name'`, and value could be `'filename'`, `fileobj` just like in the following way:

```
{'name' : file-like-objects} or
{'name': ('filename',  fileobj)}
```

The example is as follows:

```
>>> url = 'some api endpoint'
>>> files = {'file': open('plan.csv', 'rb')}
>>> r = requests.post(url, files=files)


We can access the response using 'r.text'.
>>>   r.text
{
    ...
    "files": {
        "file": "< some data … >"
        },
    ….
}
```

In the former example, we didn't specify the content-type or headers. To add to that, we have the capability to set the name for the file we are uploading:

```
>>> url = 'some url'
>>> files = {'file': ('plan.csv', open('plan.csv', 'rb'), 'application/
csv', {'Expires': '0'})}
>>> r = requests.post(url, files)
>>> r.text
{
    ...
    "files"
        "file": "< data...>"
        },
    ...
}
```

We can also send strings to be received as files in the following way:

```
>>> url = 'some url'
>>> files = {'file' : ('plan.csv', 'some, strings, to, send')}
>>> r.text
{
    ...
    "files": {
        "file": "some, strings, to, send"
    },
    ...
}
```

Looking up built-in response status codes

Status codes are helpful in letting us know the result, once a request is sent. To know about this, we can use status_code:

```
>>> r = requests.get('http://google.com')
>>> r.status_code
200
```

To make it much easier to deal with status_codes, Requests has got a built-in status code lookup object which serves as an easy reference. We must compare the requests.codes.ok with r.status_code to achieve this. If the result turns out to be True, then it's 200 status code, and if it's False, it's not. We can also compare the r.status.code with requests.codes.ok, requests.code.all_good to get the lookup work.

```
>>> r = requests.get('http://google.com')
>>> r.status_code == requests.codes.ok
True
```

Now, let's try checking with a URL that is non-existent.

```
>>> r = requests.get('http://google.com/404')
>>> r.status_code == requests.codes.ok
False
```

We have got the facility to deal with the bad `requests` like 4XX and 5XX type of errors, by notifying with the error codes. This can be accomplished by using `Response.raise_for_status()`.

Let us try this by sending a bad request first:

```
>>> bad_request = requests.get('http://google.com/404')
>>> bad_request.status_code
404
>>>bad_request.raise_for_status()
------------------------------------------------------------------------
---
HTTPError                                 Traceback (most recent call last)
----> bad_request..raise_for_status()

File "requests/models.py",  in raise_for_status(self)
    771
    772          if http_error_msg:
--> 773              raise HTTPError(http_error_msg, response=self)
    774
    775      def close(self):


HTTPError: 404 Client Error: Not Found
```

Now if we try a working URL, we get nothing in response, which is a sign of success:

```
>>> bad_request = requests.get('http://google.com')
>>> bad_request.status_code
200
>>> bad_request.raise_for_status()
>>>
```

Viewing response headers

The server response header helps us to know about the software used by the origin server to handle the request. We can access the server response headers using r.headers:

```
>>> r = requests.get('http://google.com')
>>> r.headers
CaseInsensitiveDict({'alternate-protocol': '80:quic', 'x-xss-protection':
'1; mode=block', 'transfer-encoding': 'chunked', 'set-cookie': 'PREF=ID=3
c5de2786273fce1:FF=0:TM=1410378309:LM=1410378309:S=DirRRD4dRAxp2Q_3; .....
```

Requests for Comments (RFC) 7230 says that HTTP header names are not case-sensitive. This gives us a capability to access the headers with both capital and lower-case letters.

```
>>> r.headers['Content-Type']
'text/html; charset=ISO-8859-1'


>>>  r.headers.get('content-type')
'text/html; charset=ISO-8859-1'
```

Accessing cookies with Requests

We can access cookies from the response, if they exist:

```
>>> url = 'http://somewebsite/some/cookie/setting/url'
>>> r = requests.get(url)


>>> r.cookies['some_cookie_name']
'some_cookie_value'
```

We can send our own cookies, as shown in the following example:

```
>>> url = 'http://httpbin.org/cookies'
>>> cookies = dict(cookies_are='working')


>>> r = requests.get(url, cookies=cookies)
>>> r.text
'{"cookies": {"cookies_are": "working"}}'
```

Tracking redirection of the request using request history

Sometimes the URL that we are accessing may have been moved or it might get redirected to some other location. We can track them using Requests. The response object's history property can be used to track the redirection. Requests can accomplish location redirection with every verb except with HEAD. The `Response.history` list contains the objects of the Requests that were generated in order to complete the request.

```
>>> r = requests.get('http:google.com')
>>> r.url
u'http://www.google.co.in/?gfe_rd=cr&ei=rgMSVOjiFKnV8ge37YGgCA'
>>> r.status_code
200
>>> r.history
(<Response [302]>,)
```

In the preceding example, when we tried sending a request to `'www.google.com'`, we got the `r.history` value as `302` which means the URL has been redirected to some other location. The `r.url` shows us the proof here, with the redirection URL.

If we don't want Requests to handle redirections, or if we are using POST, GET, PUT, PATCH, OPTIONS, or DELETE, we can set the value of `allow_redirects=False`, so that redirection handling gets disabled.

```
>>> r = requests.get('http://google.com', allow_redirects=False)
>>> r.url
u'http://google.com/'
>> r.status_code
302
>>> r.history
[ ]
```

In the preceding example, we used the parameter `allow_redirects=False`, which resulted the `r.url` without any redirection in the URL and the `r.history` as empty.

If we are using the head to access the URL, we can facilitate redirection.

```
>>> r = requests.head('http://google.com', allow_redirects=True)
>>> r.url
```

```
u'http://www.google.co.in/?gfe_rd=cr&ei=RggSVMbIKajV8gfxzID4Ag'
>>> r.history
(<Response [302]>,)
```

In this example, we tried accessing the URL with head and the parameter `allow_redirects` enabled which resulted us the URL redirected.

Using timeout to keep productive usage in check

Take a case in which we are trying to access a response which is taking too much time. If we don't want to get the process moving forward and give out an exception if it exceeds a specific amount of time, we can use the parameter `timeout`.

When we use the `timeout` parameter, we are telling Requests not to wait for a response after some specific time period. If we use `timeout`, it's not equivalent to defining a time limit on the whole response download. It's a good practice to raise an exception if no bytes have been acknowledged on the underlying socket for the stated `timeout` in seconds.

```
>>> requests.get('http://google.com', timeout=0.03)
-------------------------------------------------------------------------
---
Timeout                                      Traceback (most recent call
last)
.......
.......
Timeout: HTTPConnectionPool(host='google.com', port=80): Read timed\ out.
(read timeout=0.03)
```

In this example we have specified the `timeout` value as `0.03` in which the timeout has been exceeded to bring us the response and so it resulted us the `timeout` exception. The timeout may occur in two different cases:

- The request getting timed out while attempting to connect to the server that is in a remote place.
- The request getting timed out if the server did not send the whole response in the allocated time period.

Errors and exceptions

Different types of errors and exceptions will be raised when something goes wrong in the process of sending a request and getting back a response. Some of them are as follows:

- HTTPError: When there are invalid HTTP responses, Requests will raise an HTTPError exception

- ConnectionError: If there is a network problem, such as refused connection and DNS failure, Requests will raise a ConnectionError exception

- Timeout: If the request gets timed out, this exception will be raised

- TooManyRedirects: If the request surpasses the configured number of maximum redirections, this type of exception is raised

Other types of exception that come in to the picture are Missing schema Exception, InvalidURL, ChunkedEncodingError, and ContentDecodingError and so on.

This example has been taken from Request documents available at http://docs.python-requests.org/en/latest/user/quickstart/#errors-and-exceptions.

Summary

In this chapter, we covered a few basic topics. We learned why Requests is better than urllib2, how to make a simple request, different types of response contents, adding custom headers to our Requests, dealing with form encoded data, using the status code lookups, locating request redirection location and about timeouts.

In the next chapter, we will learn the advanced concepts in Requests, in depth, which will help us to use the Requests library flexibly, according to the requirements.

2
Digging Deep into Requests

In this chapter, we are going to deal with advanced topics in the Requests module. There are many more features in the Requests module that makes the interaction with the web a cakewalk. Let us get to know more about different ways to use Requests module which helps us to understand the ease of using it.

In a nutshell, we will cover the following topics:

- Persisting parameters across requests using Session objects
- Revealing the structure of request and response
- Using prepared requests
- Verifying SSL certificate with Requests
- Body Content Workflow
- Using generator for sending chunk encoded requests
- Getting the request method arguments with event hooks
- Iterating over streaming API
- Self-describing the APIs with link headers
- Transport Adapter

Persisting parameters across Requests using Session objects

The Requests module contains a `session` object, which has the capability to persist settings across the requests. Using this `session` object, we can persist cookies, we can create prepared requests, we can use the keep-alive feature and do many more things. The Session object contains all the methods of Requests API such as GET, POST, PUT, DELETE and so on. Before using all the capabilities of the Session object, let us get to know how to use sessions and persist cookies across requests.

Let us use the session method to get the resource.

```
>>> import requests
>>> session = requests.Session()
>>> response = requests.get("https://google.co.in", cookies={"new-cookie-identifier": "1234abcd"})
```

In the preceding example, we created a `session` object with `requests` and its `get` method is used to access a web resource.

The `cookie` value which we had set in the previous example will be accessible using `response.request.headers`.

```
>>> response.request.headers
CaseInsensitiveDict({'Cookie': 'new-cookie-identifier=1234abcd', 'Accept-Encoding': 'gzip, deflate, compress', 'Accept': '*/*', 'User-Agent': 'python-requests/2.2.1 CPython/2.7.5+ Linux/3.13.0-43-generic'})
>>> response.request.headers['Cookie']
'new-cookie-identifier=1234abcd'
```

With `session` object, we can specify some default values of the properties, which needs to be sent to the server using GET, POST, PUT and so on. We can achieve this by specifying the values to the properties like `headers`, `auth` and so on, on a `Session` object.

```
>>> session.params = {"key1": "value", "key2": "value2"}
>>> session.auth = ('username', 'password')
>>> session.headers.update({'foo': 'bar'})
```

In the preceding example, we have set some default values to the properties — params, auth, and `headers` using the `session` object. We can override them in the subsequent request, as shown in the following example, if we want to:

```
>>> session.get('http://mysite.com/new/url', headers={'foo': 'new-bar'})
```

Revealing the structure of a request and response

A Requests object is the one which is created by the user when he/she tries to interact with a web resource. It will be sent as a prepared request to the server and does contain some parameters which are optional. Let us have an eagle eye view on the parameters:

- `Method`: This is the HTTP method to be used to interact with the web service. For example: GET, POST, PUT.
- `URL`: The web address to which the request needs to be sent.
- `headers`: A dictionary of headers to be sent in the request.
- `files`: This can be used while dealing with the multipart upload. It's the dictionary of files, with key as file name and value as file object.
- `data`: This is the body to be attached to the `request.json`. There are two cases that come in to the picture here:
  - If `json` is provided, `content-type` in the header is changed to `application/json` and at this point, `json` acts as a body to the request.
  - In the second case, if both `json` and `data` are provided together, `data` is silently ignored.
- `params`: A dictionary of URL parameters to append to the URL.
- `auth`: This is used when we need to specify the authentication to the request. It's a tuple containing username and password.
- `cookies`: A dictionary or a cookie jar of cookies which can be added to the request.
- `hooks`: A dictionary of callback hooks.

A Response object contains the response of the server to a HTTP request. It is generated once Requests gets a response back from the server. It contains all of the information returned by the server and also stores the Request object we created originally.

Whenever we make a call to a server using the `requests`, two major transactions are taking place in this context which are listed as follows:

- We are constructing a Request object which will be sent out to the server to request a resource
- A Response object is generated by the `requests` module

Now, let us look at an example of getting a resource from Python's official site.

```
>>> response = requests.get('https://python.org')
```

In the preceding line of code, a `requests` object gets constructed and will be sent to `'https://python.org'`. Thus obtained Requests object will be stored in the `response.request` variable. We can access the headers of the Request object which was sent off to the server in the following way:

```
>>> response.request.headers
```

CaseInsensitiveDict({'Accept-Encoding': 'gzip, deflate, compress', 'Accept': '*/*', 'User-Agent': 'python-requests/2.2.1 CPython/2.7.5+ Linux/3.13.0-43-generic'})

The headers returned by the server can be accessed with its 'headers' attribute as shown in the following example:

```
>>> response.headers
```

CaseInsensitiveDict({'content-length': '45950', 'via': '1.1 varnish', 'x-cache': 'HIT', 'accept-ranges': 'bytes', 'strict-transport-security': 'max-age=63072000; includeSubDomains', 'vary': 'Cookie', 'server': 'nginx', 'age': '557','content-type': 'text/html; charset=utf-8', 'public-key-pins': 'max-age=600; includeSubDomains; ..)

The `response` object contains different attributes like `_content`, `status_code`, `headers`, `url`, `history`, `encoding`, `reason`, `cookies`, `elapsed`, `request`.

```
>>> response.status_code
200
>>> response.url
u'https://www.python.org/'
>>> response.elapsed
datetime.timedelta(0, 1, 904954)
>>> response.reason
'OK'
```

Using prepared Requests

Every request we send to the server turns to be a `PreparedRequest` by default. The `request` attribute of the `Response` object which is received from an API call or a session call is actually the `PreparedRequest` that was used.

There might be cases in which we ought to send a request which would incur an extra step of adding a different parameter. Parameters can be `cookies`, `files`, `auth`, `timeout` and so on. We can handle this extra step efficiently by using the combination of sessions and prepared requests. Let us look at an example:

```
>>> from requests import Request, Session
>>> header = {}
>>> request = Request('get', 'some_url', headers=header)
```

We are trying to send a `get` request with a header in the previous example. Now, take an instance where we are planning to send the request with the same method, URL, and headers, but we want to add some more parameters to it. In this condition, we can use the session method to receive complete session level state to access the parameters of the initial sent request. This can be done by using the `session` object.

```
>>> from requests import Request, Session
>>> session = Session()
>>> request1 = Request('GET', 'some_url', headers=header)
```

Now, let us prepare a request using the `session` object to get the values of the `session` level state:

```
>>> prepare = session.prepare_request(request1)
```

We can send the request object `request` with more parameters now, as follows:

```
>>> response = session.send(prepare, stream=True, verify=True)
200
```

Voila! Huge time saving!

The `prepare` method prepares the complete request with the supplied parameters. In the previous example, the `prepare_request` method was used. There are also some other methods like `prepare_auth`, `prepare_body`, `prepare_cookies`, `prepare_headers`, `prepare_hooks`, `prepare_method`, `prepare_url` which are used to create individual properties.

Verifying an SSL certificate with Requests

Requests provides the facility to verify an SSL certificate for HTTPS requests. We can use the `verify` argument to check whether the host's SSL certificate is verified or not.

Let us consider a website which has got no SSL certificate. We shall send a GET request with the argument `verify` to it.

The syntax to send the request is as follows:

```
requests.get('no ssl certificate site', verify=True)
```

As the website doesn't have an SSL certificate, it will result an error similar to the following:

```
requests.exceptions.ConnectionError: ('Connection aborted.', error(111, 'Connection refused'))
```

Let us verify the SSL certificate for a website which is certified. Consider the following example:

```
>>> requests.get('https://python.org', verify=True)
<Response [200]>
```

In the preceding example, the result was `200`, as the mentioned website is SSL certified one.

If we do not want to verify the SSL certificate with a request, then we can put the argument `verify=False`. By default, the value of `verify` will turn to `True`.

Body Content Workflow

Take an instance where a continuous stream of data is being downloaded when we make a request. In this situation, the client has to listen to the server continuously until it receives the complete data. Consider the case of accessing the content from the response first and the worry about the body next. In the above two situations, we can use the parameter `stream`. Let us look at an example:

```
>>> requests.get("https://pypi.python.org/packages/source/F/Flask/Flask-0.10.1.tar.gz", stream=True)
```

If we make a request with the parameter `stream=True`, the connection remains open and only the headers of the response will be downloaded. This gives us the capability to fetch the content whenever we need by specifying the conditions like the number of bytes of data.

The syntax is as follows:

```
if int(request.headers['content_length']) < TOO_LONG:
content = r.content
```

By setting the parameter `stream=True` and by accessing the response as a file-like object that is `response.raw`, if we use the method `iter_content`, we can iterate over `response.data`. This will avoid reading of larger responses at once.

The syntax is as follows:

```
iter_content(chunk_size=size in bytes, decode_unicode=False)
```

In the same way, we can iterate through the content using `iter_lines` method which will iterate over the response data one line at a time.

The syntax is as follows:

```
iter_lines(chunk_size = size in bytes, decode_unicode=None,
delimitter=None)
```

 The important thing that should be noted while using the `stream` parameter is it doesn't release the connection when it is set as `True`, unless all the data is consumed or `response.close` is executed.

The Keep-alive facility

As the `urllib3` supports the reuse of the same socket connection for multiple requests, we can send many requests with one socket and receive the responses using the keep-alive feature in the `Requests` library.

Within a session, it turns to be automatic. Every request made within a session automatically uses the appropriate connection by default. The connection that is being used will be released after all the data from the body is read.

Streaming uploads

A file-like object which is of massive size can be streamed and uploaded using the `Requests` library. All we need to do is to supply the contents of the stream as a value to the `data` attribute in the `request` call as shown in the following lines.

The syntax is as follows:

```
with open('massive-body', 'rb') as file:
    requests.post('http://example.com/some/stream/url',
                  data=file)
```

Using generator for sending chunk encoded Requests

Chunked transfer encoding is a mechanism for transferring data in an HTTP request. With this mechanism, the data is sent in a series of chunks. Requests supports chunked transfer encoding, for both outgoing and incoming requests. In order to send a chunk encoded request, we need to supply a generator for your body.

The usage is shown in the following example:

```
>>> def generator():
...     yield "Hello "
...     yield "World!"
...
>>> requests.post('http://example.com/some/chunked/url/path',
                data=generator())
```

Getting the request method arguments with event hooks

We can alter the portions of the request process signal event handling using hooks. For example, there is hook named `response` which contains the response generated from a request. It is a dictionary which can be passed as a parameter to the request. The syntax is as follows:

```
hooks = {hook_name: callback_function, … }
```

The `callback_function` parameter may or may not return a value. When it returns a value, it is assumed that it is to replace the data that was passed in. If the callback function doesn't return any value, there won't be any effect on the data.

Here is an example of a callback function:

```
>>> def print_attributes(request, *args, **kwargs):
...     print(request.url)
...     print(request .status_code)
...     print(request .headers)
```

If there is an error in the execution of `callback_function`, you'll receive a warning message in the standard output.

Now let us print some of the attributes of the request, using the preceding `callback_function`:

```
>>> requests.get('https://www.python.org/',
                 hooks=dict(response=print_attributes))
https://www.python.org/
200
CaseInsensitiveDict({'content-type': 'text/html; ...})
<Response [200]>
```

Iterating over streaming APIs

Streaming API tends to keep the request open allowing us to collect the stream data in real time. While dealing with a continuous stream of data, to ensure that none of the messages being missed from it we can take the help of `iter_lines()` in Requests. The `iter_lines()` iterates over the response data line by line. This can be achieved by setting the parameter stream as `True` while sending the request.

 It's better to keep in mind that it's not always safe to call the `iter_lines()` function as it may result in loss of received data.

Consider the following example taken from `http://docs.python-requests.org/en/latest/user/advanced/#streaming-requests`:

```
>>> import json
>>> import requests
>>> r = requests.get('http://httpbin.org/stream/4', stream=True)
>>> for line in r.iter_lines():
...     if line:
...         print(json.loads(line) )
```

In the preceding example, the response contains a stream of data. With the help of `iter_lines()`, we tried to print the data by iterating through every line.

Encodings

As specified in the HTTP protocol (RFC 7230), applications can request the server to return the HTTP responses in an encoded format. The process of encoding turns the response content into an understandable format which makes it easy to access it. When the HTTP header fails to return the type of encoding, Requests will try to assume the encoding with the help of `chardet`.

If we access the response headers of a request, it does contain the keys of `content-type`. Let us look at a response header's `content-type`:

```
>>> re = requests.get('http://google.com')
>>> re.headers['content-type']
 'text/html; charset=ISO-8859-1'
```

In the preceding example the content type contains `'text/html; charset=ISO-8859-1'`. This happens when the Requests finds the `charset` value to be `None` and the `'content-type'` value to be `'Text'`.

It follows the protocol RFC 7230 to change the value of `charset` to `ISO-8859-1` in this type of a situation. In case we are dealing with different types of encodings like `'utf-8'`, we can explicitly specify the encoding by setting the property to `Response.encoding`.

HTTP verbs

Requests support the usage of the full range of HTTP verbs which are defined in the following table. To most of the supported verbs, `'url'` is the only argument that must be passed while using them.

Method	Description
GET	GET method requests a representation of the specified resource. Apart from retrieving the data, there will be no other effect of using this method.
	Definition is given as `requests.get(url, **kwargs)`
POST	The POST verb is used for the creation of new resources. The submitted `data` will be handled by the server to a specified resource.
	Definition is given as `requests.post(url, data=None, json=None, **kwargs)`
PUT	This method uploads a representation of the specified URI. If the URI is not pointing to any resource, the server can create a new object with the given `data` or it will modify the existing resource.
	Definition is given as `requests.put(url, data=None, **kwargs)`
DELETE	This is pretty easy to understand. It is used to delete the specified resource.
	Definition is given as `requests.delete(url, **kwargs)`
HEAD	This verb is useful for retrieving meta-information written in response headers without having to fetch the response body.
	Definition is given as `requests.head(url, **kwargs)`

Method	Description
OPTIONS	OPTIONS is a HTTP method which returns the HTTP methods that the server supports for a specified URL. Definition is given as `requests.options(url, **kwargs)`
PATCH	This method is used to apply partial modifications to a resource. Definition is given as `requests.patch(url, data=None, **kwargs)`

Self-describing the APIs with link headers

Take a case of accessing a resource in which the information is accommodated in different pages. If we need to approach the next page of the resource, we can make use of the link headers. The link headers contain the meta data of the requested resource, that is the next page information in our case.

```
>>> url = "https://api.github.com/search/code?q=addClass+user:mozilla&page=1&per_page=4"
>>> response = requests.head(url=url)
>>> response.headers['link']
'<https://api.github.com/search/code?q=addClass+user%3Amozilla&page=2&per_page=4>; rel="next", <https://api.github.com/search/code?q=addClass+user%3Amozilla&page=250&per_page=4>; rel="last"
```

In the preceding example, we have specified in the URL that we want to access page number one and it should contain four records. The Requests automatically parses the link headers and updates the information about the next page. When we try to access the link header, it showed the output with the values of the page and the number of records per page.

Transport Adapter

It is used to provide an interface for Requests sessions to connect with HTTP and HTTPS. This will help us to mimic the web service to fit our needs. With the help of Transport Adapters, we can configure the request according to the HTTP service we opt to use. Requests contains a Transport Adapter called **HTTPAdapter** included in it.

Consider the following example:

```
>>> session = requests.Session()
>>> adapter = requests.adapters.HTTPAdapter(max_retries=6)
>>> session.mount("http://google.co.in", adapter)
```

In this example, we created a request session in which every request we make retries only six times, when the connection fails.

Summary

In this chapter, we learnt about creating sessions and using the session with different criteria. We also looked deeply into HTTP verbs and using proxies. We learnt about streaming requests, dealing with SSL certificate verifications and streaming responses. We also got to know how to use prepared requests, link headers and chunk encoded requests.

In the next chapter, we will learn about various types of authentication and ways to use them with Requests.

3
Authenticating with Requests

Requests supports diverse kinds of authentication procedures, and it is built in such a way that the method of authentication feels like a cakewalk. In this chapter, we opt to throw light on various types of authentication procedures that are used by various tech giants for accessing the web resources.

We will cover the following topics:

- Basic authentication
- Digest authentication
- Kerberos authentication
- OAuth authentication
- Custom authentication

Basic authentication

Basic authentication is a popular, industry-standard scheme of authentication, which is specified in HTTP 1.0. This method makes use of a user-ID and password submitted by the user to get authenticated. The submitted user-ID and password are encoded using Base64 encoding standards and transmitted across HTTP. The server gives access to the user only if the user-ID and the password are valid. The following are the advantages of using basic authentication:

- The main advantage of using this scheme is that it is supported by most of the web browsers and servers. Even though it is simple and straightforward, it does have some disadvantages. Though all the credentials are encoded and transferred in the requests, they are not encrypted which makes the process insecure. One way to overcome this problem is by using SSL support while initiating a secure session.

- Secondly, the credentials persist on the server until the end of the browser session, which may lead to the seizure of the resources. And also, this authentication process is wide open to **Cross Site Request Forgery (CSRF)** attacks, as the browser automatically sends the credentials of the user in the subsequent requests.

The basic authentication flow contains two steps:

1. If a requested resource needs authentication, the server returns http 401 response containing a WWW-Authenticate header.

2. If the user sends another request with the user ID and password in the Authorization header, the server processes the submitted credentials and gives the access.

You can see this in the following diagram:

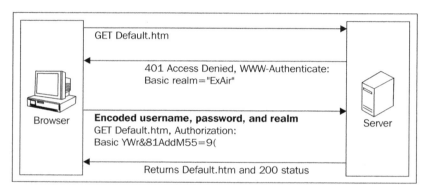

Using basic authentication with Requests

We can use the requests module to send a request to undergo basic authentication very easily. The process can be seen as follows:

```
>>> from requests.auth import HTTPBasicAuth
```

```
>>> requests.get('https://demo.example.com/resource/path',
auth=HTTPBasicAuth('user-ID', 'password'))
```

In the preceding lines of code, we performed basic authentication by creating an HTTPBasicAuth object; then we passed it to the auth parameter, which will be submitted to the server. If the submitted credentials gets authenticated successfully, the server returns a 200 (Successful) response, otherwise, it will return a 401 (Unauthorized) response.

Digest authentication

Digest authentication is one of the well known HTTP authentication schemes, which were introduced to overcome most of the drawbacks of basic authentication. This type of authentication makes use of `user-ID` and `password` just like Basic authentication, but the major difference comes in the picture, when the credentials get transferred to the server.

Digest authentication increases the security of the credentials by going an extra mile with the concept of cryptographic encryption. When the user submits the password for the sake of authentication, the browser will apply an MD5 hashing scheme on it. The crux of the process lies in using nonce values (pseudo-random numbers) while encrypting the password which decreases the replay attacks.

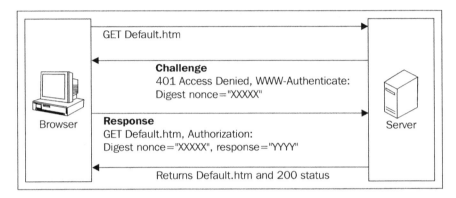

This type of authentication gains more strength, as the password in this encryption is not used in the form of plain text. The cracking of the password hashes becomes difficult in digest authentication with the use of a nonce, which counters the chosen plain text attacks.

Even though Digest authentication overcomes most of the drawbacks of Basic authentication, it does have some disadvantages. This scheme of authentication is vulnerable to man-in-the-middle attacks. It reduces the flexibility of storing the password in the password's database, as all the well designed password databases use other encryption methods to store them.

Using Digest authentication with Requests

Using Digest authentication with `requests` is very simple. Let us see how it's done:

```
>>> from requests.auth import HTTPDigestAuth
>>> requests.get('https://demo.example.com/resource/path',
auth=HTTPDigestAuth('user-ID', 'password'))
```

In the preceding lines of code, we carried out digest authentication by creating an `HTTPDigestAuth` object and setting it to the 'auth' parameter which will be submitted to the server. If the submitted credentials gets authenticated successfully, the server returns a `200` response, otherwise, it will return a `401` response.

Kerberos authentication

Kerberos is a type of Network authentication protocol, which uses a secret key cryptography to communicate between the client and the server. It was developed at MIT to mitigate many security problems like replay attacks and spying. It makes use of *tickets* to provide authentication for the server-side resources. It followed the idea of avoiding additional logins (single sign on) and storing the passwords at a centralized location.

In a nutshell, the authentication server, the ticket granting server and the host machine act as the leading cast in the process of authentication.

- **Authentication Server**: A server-side application which aids in the process of authentication by making the use of submitted credentials of a user
- **Ticket Granting Server**: A logical **key distribution center** (**KDC**) which validates the tickets
- **Host Machine**: A server which accepts the requests and provides the resources

You can see this in the following diagram:

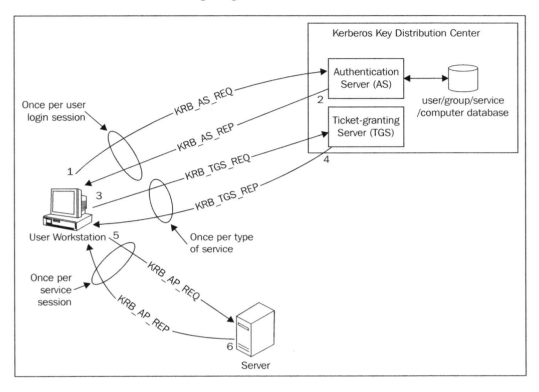

Authentication with Kerberos takes place in the following steps:

1. When a person logs into his machine with the credentials, a request will be sent to **ticket granting ticket (TGT)**.

2. If the verification of the user turns out to be true, when checked from the user database, a session key and a TGT will be created by the authentication server (AS).

3. Thus, the obtained TGT and session key will be sent back to the user in the form of two messages, in which TGT will be encrypted with the ticket granting the server's secret key. The session key will be encrypted with the client secret key and it contains a time stamp, life time, TGS name and TGS session key.

4. The user on the other end, after receiving the two messages, uses the client secret key that is, the user's password to decrypt the messages of the session key. The TGT cannot be decrypted without the TGS secret key.

5. With the available information of the `session` key and the TGT, the user can send a request for accessing the service. The request contains two messages and some information at this point. In the two messages, one is an encrypted message, containing a user ID and timestamp. The other is a decrypted message, containing the HTTP service name and the life time of the ticket. With the above two messages, an authenticator and TGT will be sent to the ticket granting server.

6. The messages and the information (Authenticator and TGT) will be received by the TGS, and it will check for the credibility of the HTTP service from the KDC database and decrypt both the authenticator and the TGT. Once everything goes fine, the TGS tries to verify some important parts like client ID, time stamp, lifetime of TGT and authenticator. If the verification turns out to be successful, then the TGS generates an encrypted HTTP service ticket, HTTP service name, time stamp, information about the ticket validity and the session key of HTTP service. All of the preceding ones will be encrypted by the HTTP Service session key and will be sent back to the user.

7. Now, the user receives the information and decrypts it with the TGS session key that he/she received in the earlier step.

8. In the next step, to access the HTTP service, the user sends an encrypted HTTP service ticket and an authenticator which is encrypted with the HTTP service session key to the HTTP service. The HTTP service uses its secret key to decrypt the ticket and takes hold of the HTTP service session key. With the acquired HTTP service session key, it decrypts the authenticator and verifies the client ID time stamp, lifetime of ticket, and so on.

9. If the verification turns out to be successful, the HTTP service sends an authenticator message with its ID and time stamp to confirm its identity to the user. The user's machine verifies the authenticator by making use of HTTP service session key and identifies the user as an authenticated one who accesses the HTTP service. From then onwards, the HTTP service can be accessed by the user without any bumps, until the session key expires.

Kerberos is a secure protocol as the passwords from the user can never be sent as plain text. As the process of authentication takes place with the agreement of both the client and the server through encryption and decryption, it turns out to be a rigid one to break to some extent. The other advantage comes from its capability to give server access to the user until the session key expires without reentering the password.

Kerberos does have some disadvantages:

- The server must be continuously available for the verification of the tickets which may result in blocking, if the server goes down.

- User's keys are saved on a central server. A breach of this server may compromise security for the whole infrastructure.

- Kerberos necessitates a heavy infrastructure, which means a simple web server is not sufficient.

- The setup and the administration of Kerberos requires specialized skills.

Using Kerberos authentication with Requests

Requests takes the support of the `requests-kerberos` library for the purpose of authentication. For this reason, we should first install the `requests-kerberos` module.

```
>>> pip install 'requests-kerberos'
```

Let's have a look at the syntax:

```
>>> import requests
>>> from requests.kerberos import HTTPKerberosAuth
>>> requests.get('https://demo.example.com/resource/path',
auth=HTTTPKerberosAuth())
```

In the preceding lines of code, we carried out Kerberos authentication by creating an `HTTPKerberosAuth` object and setting it to the `auth` parameter which will be submitted to the server.

OAuth authentication

OAuth is an open standard authorization protocol, which allows client applications a *secure delegated access* to the user accounts on third party services such as Google, Twitter, GitHub and so on. In this topic, we are going to introduce the two versions:- OAuth 1.0 and OAuth 2.0.

OAuth 1.0

OAuth authentication protocol came up with an idea of mitigating the usage of passwords, replacing them with secure handshakes with API calls between the applications. This was developed by a small group of web developers who are inspired by OpenID.

Here are the Key terms used in the process of OAuth authentication.

- **Consumer**: The HTTP Client who can make authenticated requests
- **Service Provider**: The HTTP Server, which deals with the requests of OAuth
- **User**: A person who has the control over the protected resources on the HTTP Server
- **Consumer Key and Secret**: Identifiers which have the capability to authenticate and authorize a request
- **Request Token and Secret**: Credentials used to gain authorization from the user
- **Access Token and Secret**: Credentials to get access to the protected resources of the user

You can see this in the following diagram:

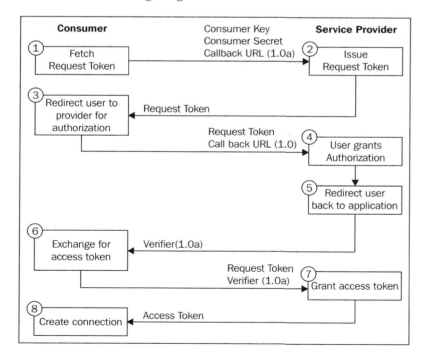

Initially, the client application asks the service provider to grant a request token. A user can be identified as an approved user by taking the credibility of the request token. It also helps in acquiring the access token with which the client application can access the service provider's resources.

In the second step, the service provider receives the request and issues request token, which will be sent back to the client application. Later, the user gets redirected to the service provider's authorization page along with the request token received before as an argument.

In the next step, the user grants permission to use the consumer application. Now, the service provider returns the user back to the client application, where the application accepts an authorized request token and gives back an access token. Using the access token, the user will gain an access to the application.

Using OAuth 1.0 authentication with Requests

The `requests_oauthlib` is a an optional library for `oauth` which is not included in the Requests module. For this reason, we should install `requests_oauthlib` separately.

Let us take a look at the syntax:

```
>>> import requests
>>> from requests_oauthlib import OAuth1
>>> auth = OAuth1('<consumer key>', '<consumer secret>',
...                '<user oauth token>', '<user oauth token secret>')
>>> requests.get('https://demo.example.com/resource/path', auth=auth)
```

OAuth 2.0

OAuth 2.0 is next in line to OAuth 1.0 which has been developed to overcome the drawbacks of its predecessor. In modern days, OAuth 2.0 has been used vividly in almost all leading web services. Due to its ease of use with more security, it has attracted many people. The beauty of OAuth 2.0 comes from its simplicity and its capability to provide specific authorization methods for different types of application like web, mobile and desktop.

Basically, there are four workflows available while using OAuth 2.0, which are also called **grant types**. They are:

1. **Authorization code grant**: This is basically used in web applications for the ease of authorization and secure resource delegation.

2. **Implicit grant**: This flow is used to provide OAuth authorization in Mobile Applications.

3. **Resource owner password credentials grant**: This type of grant is used for applications using trusted clients.

4. **Client credentials grant**: This type of grant is used in machine to machine authentication. An in-depth explanation about grant types is out of the scope of this book.

OAuth 2.0 came up with capabilities which could overcome the concerns of OAuth 1.0. The process of using signatures to verify the credibility of API requests has been replaced by the use of SSL in OAuth 2.0. It came up with the idea of supporting different types of flow for different environments ranging from web to mobile applications. Also, the concept of refresh tokens has been introduced to increase the security.

Let us take a look at the usage:

```
>>> from requests_oauthlib import OAuth2Session
>>> client = OAuth2Session('<client id>', token='token')
>>> resp = client.get('https://demo.example.com/resource/path')
```

Custom authentication

Requests also provides the ability to write a new or custom authentication based on the user's needs and flexibility. It is equipped with requests.auth.AuthBase class which is a base class for all the authentication types. This can be achieved by implementing the custom authentication in the __call__() of requests.auth.AuthBase.

Let us take a look at its syntax:

```
>>> import requests
>>> class CustomAuth(requests.auth.AuthBase):
...     def __call__(self, r):
...         # Custom Authentication Implemention
```

```
...          return r
...
>>> requests.get('https://demo.example.com/resource/path',
... auth=CustomAuth())
```

Summary

In this chapter, we gained knowledge of various types of authentication like Basic authentication, Digest authentication, Kerberos authentication, OAuth 1.0 authentication and OAuth 2.0 authentication which are supported by Requests. Later, we got an idea of how to use various types of authentications and the flows of the process. We also learned to use our own custom authentication and gained the knowledge of making different authentications work with Requests and the ways to use them with Requests.

In the next chapter, we will be getting to know all about a handy module, HTTPretty.

4
Mocking HTTP Requests Using HTTPretty

With the `Requests` module, we gained the means to open URLs, post data, and get data from web services. Let us take an instance of building an application, which uses a RESTful API and unfortunately, the API on which the server is running is down. Even though we achieved interaction with the web using Requests, we failed this time because we got no response from the server's side. This condition may leave us irked and blocked from our progress, as we found no way of testing our code any further.

So, there came this idea of creating an HTTP request mock tool, which can serve us by mocking the web server on the client side. Even though HTTPretty is no way directly connected with Requests, we would like to introduce a mock tool which would help us in the previously mentioned case.

 [HTTP mock tool helps to mock web services by faking requests.]

We'll look at the following topics in this chapter:

- Understanding HTTPretty
- Installing HTTPretty
- Usage in detail
- Setting headers
- Working with responses

Understanding HTTPretty

HTTPretty is an HTTP client mock library for Python. The basic idea of HTTPretty is inspired by Ruby's FakeWeb, which is well known to the people from the Ruby community. HTTPretty re-implements the HTTP protocol by mimicking requests and responses.

Essentially, HTTPretty works on socket level, which gives it the inward virtue of working with most of the HTTP client libraries and it is more specifically battle tested against HTTP client libraries like `Requests`, `httplib2` and `urlib2`. So, we can mock the interactions from our Request library without any difficulty.

Here are the two cases in which HTTPretty comes to the rescue:

- The condition in which the API server is down
- The condition in which the API content has changed

Installing HTTPretty

We can install HTTPretty effortlessly from **Python Package Index (PyPi)**.

```
pip install HTTPretty
```

We will be learning many more things with examples in this process of getting used to HTTPretty; And in this course of journey we will be using libraries like mock, sure and obviously Requests. Here we go, with those installations:

```
>>> pip install requests sure mock
```

Let us take a peek at what exactly those packages deal with:

- `mock`: It is a testing library which allows us to replace parts of the system under test with mock objects
- `sure`: It is a Python library which is used to make assertions

Working with HTTPretty

There are three main steps to be followed while dealing with HTTPretty:

1. Enable HTTPretty
2. Register the uniform resource locator to HTTPretty
3. Disable HTTPretty

We should enable HTTPretty initially, so that it will apply monkey patching; that is, a dynamic replacement of the attributes of the socket module. We will be using the function `register_uri` for registering the uniform resource locator. The `register_uri` function takes `class`, `uri` and `body` as arguments:

```
method: register_uri(class, uri, body)
```

And at the end of our testing process, we should disable HTTPretty so that it doesn't alter the behavior of the other. Let us take a look at using HTTPretty with an example:

```python
import httpretty
import requests
from sure import expect


def example():
    httpretty.enable()
    httpretty.register_uri(httpretty.GET, "http://google.com/",
                           body="This is the mocked body",
                           status=201)
    response = requests.get("http://google.com/")
    expect(response.status_code).to.equal(201)
    httpretty.disable()
```

In this example, we used the `httpretty.GET` class in `register_uri` function to register the `uri` value that is `"http://google.com/"`. In the next line, we used Request to get the information from the URI and then we used the expect function to assert the expected status code. In a nutshell, the preceding code tries to mock the URI and tests whether we are getting the same status code as expected.

We can simplify the preceding code using a decorator. As in the first and third step, that is, enabling and disabling HTTPretty are same all the time, we can use a decorator so that those functions get wrapped up whenever we want them to come into the picture. The decorator looks like this: `@httpretty.activate`. The previous code example can be rewritten using a decorator in the following way:

```python
import httpretty
import requests

from sure import expect


@httpretty.activate
```

```python
def example():
    httpretty.register_uri(httpretty.GET, "http://google.com/",
                           body="This is the mocked body",
                           status=201)
    response = requests.get("http://google.com/")
    expect(response.status_code).to.equal(201)
```

Setting headers

HTTP header fields supply the necessary information about the request or response. We can mock any HTTP response header by using HTTPretty. To achieve that, we will be adding them as keyword arguments. We should keep in mind that the keys of the keyword arguments are always lower case and have underscores (_) instead of dashes.

For example, if we want to mock the server, which returns Content-Type, we can use the argument content_type. Do notice that, in the following part we are using an inexistent URL to showcase the syntax:

```python
import httpretty
import requests


from sure import expect


@httpretty.activate
def setting_header_example():
    httpretty.register_uri(httpretty.GET,
                           "http://api.example.com/some/path",
                           body='{"success": true}',
                           status=200,
                           content_type='text/json')

    response = requests.get("http://api.example.com/some/path")

    expect(response.json()).to.equal({'success': True})
    expect(response.status_code).to.equal(200)
```

Similarly, all the keyword arguments are taken by HTTPretty and changed into the RFC2616 equivalent name.

Working with responses

When we mock HTTP requests using HTTPretty, it returns an `httpretty.Response` object. We can generate the following responses through callbacks:

- Rotating Responses
- Streaming Responses
- Dynamic Responses

Rotating responses

Rotating responses are the responses we receive in a given order when we send a request to a server with the same URL and same request method. We can define as many responses as we wish with the responses argument.

The following snippet explains the mocking of Rotating Responses:

```
import httpretty
import requests


from sure import expect


@httpretty.activate
def rotating_responses_example():
    URL = "http://example.com/some/path"
    RESPONSE_1 = "This is Response 1."
    RESPONSE_2 = "This is Response 2."
    RESPONSE_3 = "This is Last Response."


    httpretty.register_uri(httpretty.GET,
                           URL,
                           responses=[
                               httpretty.Response(body=RESPONSE_1,
                                                  status=201),
                               httpretty.Response(body=RESPONSE_2,
                                                  status=202),
                               httpretty.Response(body=RESPONSE_3,
```

```
                                               status=201)])

    response_1 = requests.get(URL)
    expect(response_1.status_code).to.equal(201)
    expect(response_1.text).to.equal(RESPONSE_1)

    response_2 = requests.get(URL)
    expect(response_2.status_code).to.equal(202)
    expect(response_2.text).to.equal(RESPONSE_2)

    response_3 = requests.get(URL)
    expect(response_3.status_code).to.equal(201)
    expect(response_3.text).to.equal(RESPONSE_3)

    response_4 = requests.get(URL)
    expect(response_4.status_code).to.equal(201)
    expect(response_4.text).to.equal(RESPONSE_3)
```

In this example, we have registered three different responses using the responses argument with the `httpretty.register_uri` method. And then, we sent four different requests to the server with the same URI and the same method. As a result, we received the first three responses in the sequence of registration. From the fourth request, we'll get the last response defined in the responses object.

Streaming responses

Streaming responses will not have `Content-Length` header. Rather, they have a `Transfer-Encoding` header with a value of `chunked`, and a body consisting of a series of chunks you write to the socket preceded by their individual sizes. These kinds of responses are also called **Chunked Responses**.

We can mock a Streaming response by registering a generator response body:

```
import httpretty
import requests
from time import sleep
from sure import expect


def mock_streaming_repos(repos):
    for repo in repos:
```

```
        sleep(.5)
        yield repo

@httpretty.activate
def streaming_responses_example():
    URL = "https://api.github.com/orgs/python/repos"
    REPOS = ['{"name": "repo-1", "id": 1}\r\n',
             '\r\n',
             '{"name": "repo-2", "id": 2}\r\n']

    httpretty.register_uri(httpretty.GET,
                           URL,
                           body=mock_streaming_repos(REPOS),
                           streaming=True)

    response = requests.get(URL,
                            data={"track": "requests"})

    line_iter = response.iter_lines()
    for i in xrange(len(REPOS)):
        expect(line_iter.next().strip()).to.equal(REPOS[i].strip())
```

To mock a streaming response, we need to set the streaming argument to `True` while registering `uri`. In the previous example, we mocked the streaming response using the generator `mock_streaming_repos`, which will take the list as an argument, and will yield the list item every half second.

Dynamic responses through callbacks

If the response from the API server is generated, depending on the values from the request, then we call it a Dynamic response. To mock dynamic responses based on the request, we will use a callback method as defined in the following example:

```
import httpretty
import requests

from sure import expect

@httpretty.activate
```

```
def dynamic_responses_example():
    def request_callback(method, uri, headers):
        return (200, headers, "The {} response from {}".format(method,
uri)
    httpretty.register_uri(
        httpretty.GET, "http://example.com/sample/path",
        body=request_callback)


    response = requests.get("http://example.com/sample/path")

    expect(response.text).to.equal(' http://example.com/sample/path')
```

In this example, `request_callback` method is registered while mocking the response, in order to generate dynamic response content.

Summary

In this chapter, we learnt the basic concepts related to HTTPretty. We looked at what HTTPretty is, and why we need HTTPretty. We also walked through detailed usage of the mocking library, setting headers, and mocking different types of Responses. These topics are enough for us to get started and keep the progress moving on.

In the next chapter, we will learn how to interact with the social networks like Facebook, Twitter, and reddit with the requests library.

5
Interacting with Social Media Using Requests

In this contemporary world, our lives are woven with a lot of interactions and collaborations with social media. The information that is available on the web is very valuable and it is being used by abundant resources. For instance, the news that is trending in the world can be spotted easily from a Twitter hashtag and this can be achieved by interacting with the Twitter API.

Using natural language processing, we can classify emotion of a person by grabbing the Facebook status of an account. All this stuff can be accomplished easily with the help of Requests using the concerned APIs. Requests is a perfect module, if we want to reach out API frequently, as it supports pretty much everything, like caching, redirection, proxies, and so on.

We will cover the following topics in this chapter:

- Interacting with Twitter
- Interacting with Facebook
- Interacting with reddit

API introduction

Before diving into details, let us have a quick look at what exactly is an **Application Programming Interface (API)**.

A web API is a set of rules and specifications. It assists us to communicate with different software. There are different types of APIs, and REST API is the subject matter here. **REpresentational State Transfer (REST)** is an architecture containing guidelines for building scalable web services. An API which adheres to the guidelines and conforms to the constraints of REST is called a **RESTful API**. In a nutshell, the constraints are:

- Client-server
- Stateless
- Cacheable
- Layered system
- Uniform interface
- Code on demand

Google Maps API, Twitter API, and GitHub API are various examples RESTful APIs.

Let us understand much more about an API. Take an instance of getting all tweets from Twitter with the hashtag "worldtoday" which includes the process of authenticating, sending requests and receiving responses from different URLs, and dealing with different methods. All the said processes and the procedures will be specified in the API of Twitter. By following these procedures, we can collaborate with the web smoothly.

Getting started with the Twitter API

To get started with Twitter API we should first obtain an API key. It is a code which is passed by the computer programs while calling an API. The basic purpose of the API key is that it uniquely identifies the program that it is trying to interact with. It also serves us in the process of authentication with its token.

The next step involves the process of creating an authentication request which will give us access to the Twitter account. Once we have authenticated successfully, we will be free to deal with tweets, followers, trends, searches, and stuff. Let us get to know more about the steps to follow.

Please note that, we will be using the Twitter API 1.1 version in all the examples.

Obtaining an API Key

Getting an API key is pretty simple. You need to follow the steps prescribed in the following section:

1. At first, you need to sign into the page `https://apps.twitter.com/` with your your Twitter credentials.

2. Click on **Create New App** button.

3. Now, you need to fill the following fields to set up a new application:

    ° **Name**: Specify your application name. This is used to attribute the source of a tweet and in user-facing authorization screens.

    ° **Description**: Enter a short description of your application. This will be shown when a user faces the authorization screens.

    ° **Website**: Specify your fully qualified website URL. A fully qualified URL includes http:// or https:// and will not have a trailing slash in the end (for example: `http://example.com` or `http://www.example.com`).

    ° **Callback URL**: This field answers the question — where should we return after successfully authenticating.

    ° **Developer Agreement**: Read the **Developer Agreement** carefully and then check the checkbox **Yes, I agree**.

4. Now, by clicking on **Create your Twitter application,** a new application will be created for us with the previously specified details.

5. After the successful creation, we'll be redirected to a page where the **Details** tab is selected by default. Now, select the **Keys and Access Tokens** tab. We should click on **Create my access token** button to generate our access token.

6. Lastly, make a note of the **Consumer Key (API Key), Consumer Secret (API Secret), Access Token** and **Access Token Secret**.

Creating an authentication Request

If we remember the theme of the third chapter, we learned different kinds of authentication with `requests`, such as Basic authentication, Digest authentication, and OAuth authentication. Time to apply all that stuff in real time!

Now, we will be using OAuth1 authentication to get the access to the Twitter API. In the first step of obtaining a key, we got access to Consumer key, Consumer secret, Access token and Access token secret, now we should use them to authenticate our application. The following commands show how we can accomplish the process:

```
>>> import requests
>>> from requests_oauthlib import OAuth1
>>> CONSUMER_KEY = 'YOUR_APP_CONSUMER_KEY'
>>> CONSUMER_SECRET = 'YOUR_APP_CONSUMER_SECRET'
>>> ACCESS_TOKEN = 'YOUR_APP_ACCESS_TOKEN'
>>> ACCESS_TOKEN_SECRET = 'YOUR_APP_ACCESS_TOKEN_SECRET'

>>> auth = OAuth1(CONSUMER_KEY, CONSUMER_SECRET,
...                 ACCESS_TOKEN, ACCESS_TOKEN_SECRET)
```

In the preceding lines, we have sent our keys and tokens to the API and got ourselves authenticated and stored them in the variable `auth`. Now, we can do all sorts of interactions with the API using this. Let us start to interact with the Twitter API.

 Keep in mind that, all the twitter interacting examples that are depicted after this will be using the "auth" value obtained in the previous section.

Getting your favorite tweet

Let us grab some favorite tweets of the authenticated user first. For this, we should send a request to the Twitter API to access the favorite tweets. The request can be sent with a `Resource URL` by specifying the parameters. The `Resource URL` for getting the favorite list looks like this:

```
https://api.twitter.com/1.1/favorites/list.json
```

We can also send some optional parameters to the URL like `user_id`, `screen_name`, `count`, `since_id`, `max_id`, `include_identities` to accomplish our needs. Let us get one favorite tweet now.

```
>>> favorite_tweet = requests.get('https://api.twitter.com/1.1/favorites/
list.json?count=1', auth=auth)
>>> favorite_tweet.json()
[{u'contributors': None, u'truncated': False, u'text': u'India has spent
$74 mil to reach Mars. Less than the budget of the film \u201cGravity,\
u201d $100 million.\n\n#respect\n#ISRO\n#Mangalyaan', u'in_reply_to_
status_id': None, …}]
```

In the first step, we sent a `get` request with the parameter `count` and the authentication `auth` to the resource URL. In the next step, we accessed the response within the JSON format which gave us my favorite tweet, and it is that simple.

As we have specified the count parameter as `1` in the request, we happened to see the result with one favorite tweet. By default, if we don't specify the optional parameter `count`, the request will result in `20` most recent favorite tweets.

Performing a simple search

We shall make a search with a Twitter's API now. For this, we will be making use of `Search API` of Twitter. The basic URL structure for searching has the following syntax:

```
https://api.twitter.com/1.1/search/tweets.json?q=%40twitterapi
```

It has got additional parameters like `Result type`, `Geolocation`, `language`, `Iterating in a result set`.

```
>>> search_results = requests.get('https://api.twitter.com/1.1/search/
tweets.json?q=%40python', auth=auth)
>>> search_results.json().keys()
[u'search_metadata', u'statuses']
>>> search_results.json()["search_metadata"]
{u'count': 15, u'completed_in': 0.022, u'max_id_str':
u'529975076746043392', u'since_id_str': u'0', u'next_results': u'?max_id
=527378999857532927&q=%40python&include_entities=1', u'refresh_url':
u'?since_id=529975076746043392&q=%40python&include_entities=1', u'since_
id': 0, u'query': u'%40python', u'max_id': 529975076746043392}
```

In the preceding example, we tried to search for tweets with the words `python`.

Accessing the list of followers

Let us access the followers of a specified user. By default, when we query for the list of followers, it returns the 20 most recent following users. The resource URL looks like this:

```
https://api.twitter.com/1.1/followers/list.json
```

It returns a cursored collection of user objects for users following the specified user:

```
>>> followers = requests.get('https://api.twitter.com/1.1/followers/list.
json', auth=auth)
>>> followers.json().keys()
[u'previous_cursor', u'previous_cursor_str', u'next_cursor', u'users',
u'next_cursor_str']
>>> followers.json()["users"]
[{u'follow_request_sent': False, u'profile_use_background_image': True,
u'profile_text_color': u'333333'... }]
```

Retweets

A tweet which has been reposted is called a **retweet**. To access the most recent retweets that have been authored by the authenticated user, we will be using the following URL:

```
https://api.twitter.com/1.1/statuses/retweets_of_me.json
```

The optional parameters that can be sent with it are count, since_id, max_id, trim_user, include_entites, include_user_entities

```
>>> retweets = requests.get('https://api.twitter.com/1.1/statuses/
retweets_of_me.json', auth=auth)
>>> len(retweets.json())
16
>>> retweets.json()[0]
{u'contributors': None, u'text': u'I\u2019m now available to take on new
#python #django #freelance projects. Reply for more details!', {u'screen_
name': u'vabasu', ...}}
```

Accessing available trends

Twitter trends are hashtag-driven subject matter that is popular at a specific time. Take an instance of getting a location of the available trends in Twitter. For that, we will use the following URL:

```
https://api.twitter.com/1.1/trends/available.json
```

The response of the resource URL is an array of locations in encoded form:

```
>>> available_trends = requests.get('https://api.twitter.com/1.1/trends/
available.json', auth=auth)
>>> len(available_trends.json())
467
>>> available_trends.json()[10]
{u'name': u'Blackpool', u'countryCode': u'GB', u'url': u'http://
where.yahooapis.com/v1/place/12903', u'country': u'United Kingdom',
u'parentid': 23424975, u'placeType': {u'code': 7, u'name': u'Town'},
u'woeid': 12903}
```

In the preceding lines of code, we searched for the locations of the `available_trends`. Then, we learned that the number of locations having `available_trends` is `467`. Later, we tried to access the tenth location's data and it resulted in a response with the location information which is encoded with **woeid**. This is a unique identifier called **Where on Earth ID**.

Updating user status

To update the authenticated user's current status, which is also known as tweeting, we follow the following procedure.

For each update attempt, the update text is compared with the authenticating user's recent tweets. Any attempt that would result in duplication will be blocked, resulting in a `403 error`. Therefore, a user cannot submit the same status twice in a row.

```
>>> requests.post('https://api.twitter.com/1.1/statuses/update.
json?status=This%20is%20a%20Tweet', auth=auth)
```

Interacting with Facebook

The Facebook API platform helps third-party developers like us to create our own applications and services that access data on Facebook.

Let us draw the Facebook data using the Facebook API. Facebook provides two types of APIs; that is, Graph API and Ads API. Graph API is a RESTful JSON API with which we can access the different resources from Facebook like statuses, likes, pages, photos, and so on. The Ads API basically deals with managing access to add campaigns, audiences and so on.

In this chapter, we are going to use the Facebook Graph API to interact with Facebook. It is named after its manner of representation with nodes and edges. The nodes represent the *things*, which means a user, a photo, a page; and the edges represent the connection between the things; that is page's photos, photo's comments.

 All the examples in this section will be using the Graph API version 2.2

Getting started with the Facebook API

To get started with the Facebook API, we need an opaque string called access token which is used by Facebook to identify a user, app, or page. It is followed by the steps of obtaining a key. We will be sending almost all our requests to the API at `graph.facebook.com` except the video upload stuff. The procedure to send a request takes place using the unique id of the node in the following way:

```
GET graph.facebook.com/{node-id}
```

And in the same way, we can POST in the following way:

```
POST graph.facebook.com/{node-id}
```

Obtaining a key

The tokens of Facebook API are portable and can be used to make calls from a mobile client, a web browser or from a server.

There are four different types of Access tokens:

- **User Access Token**: This is the most commonly used type of access token which needs the authorization of users. This token can be used to access the user information and to post data on the user's timeline.

- **App Access Token**: This token comes into the picture when dealing at the Application level. This token doesn't help in getting access to the user's data, but it gives access to read the stream.

- **Page Access Token**: This token can used while accessing and managing a Facebook page.

- **Client Token**: This token can be embedded in an application to get access to the app-level API's.

In this tutorial, we will be using the App access token which consists of App Id and App Secret to get access to the resources.

Follow the below steps to obtain an App access token:

1. Create an application using the developer console of Facebook at `https://developers.facebook.com/developer-console/`. Note that we should login to `http://developers.facebook.com` so that we can attain the permission to create an application.

2. Once we are done with the creation of the application, we can get the access to App Id and App Secret on the application page of our `http://developers.facebook.com` account.

That's all; obtaining a key is that simple. We don't need to create any authentication request to send messages, as opposed to how it is on Twitter. The App Id and App Secret are enough to give us permission to access the resources.

Getting a user profile

We can access the current user profile of the person who is logged into the site, using the API URL `https://graph.facebook.com/me` with a GET request. We need to pass the previously obtained access token as a parameter, while we are making any Graph API call using requests.

Firstly, we need to import the requests module and then we have to store the access token into a variable. The process works in the following way:

```
>>> import requests
>>> ACCESS_TOKEN = '231288990034554xxxxxxxxxxxxxxxx'
```

In the next step, we should send the required graph API call, in the following way:

```
>>> me = requests.get("https://graph.facebook.com/me", params={'access_
token': ACCESS_TOKEN})
```

Now, we have a `requests.Response` object called `me`. The `me.text` returns a JSON response string. To access various elements (example, `id`, `name`, `last_name`, `hometown`, `work`) of the retrieved user profile, we need to convert the `json response` string into a `json object` string. We can achieve this by calling the method `me.json()`. The `me.json.keys()` results all the keys in the dictionary:

```
>>> me.json().keys()
[u'website', u'last_name', u'relationship_status', u'locale',
u'hometown', u'quotes', u'favorite_teams', u'favorite_athletes',
u'timezone', u'education', u'id', u'first_name', u'verified',
u'political', u'languages', u'religion', u'location', u'username',
u'link', u'name', u'gender', u'work', u'updated_time', u'interested_in']
```

A user's `id` is a unique number which is used to identify the user on Facebook. We can access the current profile ID from the user profile in the following way. We'll use this ID in the subsequent examples to retrieve the current user's friends, feed and albums.

```
>>> me.json()['id']
u'10203783798823031'
>>> me.json()['name']
u'Bala Subrahmanyam Varanasi'
```

Retrieving a friends list

Let us gather the friends list of a specific user. To achieve this, we should make an API call to `https://graph.facebook.com/<user-id>/friends`, and replace the `user-id` with the value of user's ID.

Now, let us obtain the friends list of the user id that we retrieved in the former example:

```
>>> friends = requests.get("https://graph.facebook.com/10203783798823031/
friends", params={'access_token': ACCESS_TOKEN})
>>> friends.json().keys()
[u'paging', u'data']
```

The response for the API call contains a JSON object string. The friend's information is stored in the `data` attribute of the `response json` object, which is a list of friend objects containing friends' IDs and names as keys.

```
>>> len(friends.json()['data'])
32
>>> friends.json().keys()
```

```
[u'paging', u'data']
>>> friends.json()['data'][0].keys()
[u'name', u'id']
```

Retrieving feed

In order to retrieve the feed of posts which includes status updates and links published by the current user, or by others on the current user's profile, we should use the feed parameter in the request.

```
>>> feed = requests.get("https://graph.facebook.com/10203783798823031/
feed", params={'access_token': ACCESS_TOKEN})
>>> feed.json().keys()
[u'paging', u'data']
>>> len(feed.json()["data"])
24
>>> feed.json()["data"][0].keys()
[u'from', u'privacy', u'actions', u'updated_time', u'likes', u'created_
time', u'type', u'id', u'status_type']
```

In the preceding example, we sent a request to get the feeds of a specific user with user ID 10203783798823031.

Retrieving albums

Let us access the photo albums created by the current logged-in user. It can be achieved in the following way:

```
>>> albums = requests.get("https://graph.facebook.com/10203783798823031/
albums", params={'access_token': ACCESS_TOKEN})
>>> albums.json().keys()
[u'paging', u'data']
>>> len(albums.json()["data"])
13
>>> albums.json()["data"][0].keys()
[u'count', u'from', u'name', u'privacy', u'cover_photo', u'updated_time',
u'link', u'created_time', u'can_upload', u'type', u'id']
>>> albums.json()["data"][0]["name"]
u'Timeline Photos'
```

In the preceding example, we sent a request to graph API to get access to the albums of the user with `user-id` `10203783798823031`. And then we tried to access the response data through JSON.

Interacting with reddit

Reddit is one of the popular social networking, entertainment and news websites where registered members can submit content, such as text posts or direct links. It allows the registered users to vote the submissions either "up" or "down" to rank the posts on the site's pages. Each content entry is categorized by area of interest called **SUBREDDITS**.

In this section, we are going to access the reddit API directly, using the Python requests library. We are going to cover the topics of a basic overview of reddit API, getting data related to our own reddit account, and using the search API to retrieve the links.

Getting started with the reddit API

The reddit API consists of four important parts that we need to get familiar with before starting to interact with it. The four parts are:

1. **listings**: The endpoints in reddit are called listings. They contain parameters like `after`/`before`, `limit`, `count`, `show`.
2. **modhashes**: This is a token which is used to prevent the **cross site request forgery(CSRF)** exploit. We can get the modhash for us by using `GET /api/ me.json`.
3. **fullnames**: A fullname is a combination of a thing's type and its unique ID which forms a compact encoding of a globally unique ID on reddit.
4. **account**: This deals with the user's account. Using this we can register, login, set force https, update the account, update email and so on.

Registering a new account

Registering a new account on reddit is easy. First, we need to reach the reddit site— `https://www.reddit.com/`, and then have to fill up the registration form which pops up when we click on **sign in or create an account** link in the top right corner. The Registration form includes:

* **username**: Used to identify the reddit community member uniquely
* **email**: An optional field used to communicate directly with a user

- **password**: Secure password to login into the reddit platform
- **verify password**: This field should be the same as the password field
- **captcha**: This field is used to check whether the user who is trying to login is a human or a programmable bot

Let us create a new account with a username and a password of our choice. For now, leave the email field empty. We are going to add it in the next section.

In the following examples, I'm assuming that the username and password we created before are OUR_USERNAME and OUR_PASSWORD respectively.

Modifying account information

Now, let's add an email to our account's profile which we intentionally left undone while creating the account in the previous section.

1. Let us begin the process by creating a session object, which allows us to maintain certain parameters and cookies across all requests.

```
>>> import requests
>>> client = requests.session()
>>> client.headers = {'User-Agent': 'Reddit API - update profile'}
```

2. Let us create a DATA attribute with the 'user', 'passwd' and 'api type' attributes.

```
>>> DATA = {'user': 'OUR_USERNAME', 'passwd': 'OUR_PASSWORD', 'api type': 'json'}
```

3. We can access our reddit account by making a post request call to the URL— https://ssl.reddit.com/api/login with the login credentials stored in the DATA attribute.

```
>>> response = client.post('https://ssl.reddit.com/api/login', data=DATA)
```

4. The reddit api response to the above post request will be stored in the response variable. The response object contains the data and errors information as shown in the following example:

```
>>> print response.json()
{u'json': {u'errors': [], u'data': {u'need_https': False,
u'modhash': u'v4k68gabo0aba80a7fda463b5a5548120a04ffb43490f54072',
u'cookie': u'32381424,2014-11-09T13:53:30,998c473d93cfeb7abcd31ac4
57c33935a54caaa7'}}}
```

5. We need to send the `modhash` value obtained in the previous response to perform an update call to change our `email`. Now, let us call the reddit's update API as shown in the following example:

```
>>> modhash = response.json()['json']['data']['modhash']
>>> update_params = {"api_type": "json", "curpass": "OUR_
PASSWORD",
...                       "dest": "www.reddit.com", "email": "user@
example.com",
...                       "verpass": "OUR_PASSWORD", "verify": True,
'uh': modhash}
>>> r = client.post('http://www.reddit.com/api/update',
data=update_params)
```

6. The response to the update call is stored in `r`. If there are no errors, then the `status_code` will be `200` and `errors` attributes value will be an empty list as shown in the following example:

```
>>> print r.status_code
200
>>> r.text
u'{"json": {"errors": []}}'
```

7. Now, let us check whether the `email` field is set by getting info about the currently authenticated user. If the `has_mail` attribute is `True`, then we can assume that the email is successfully updated.

```
>>> me = client.get('http://www.reddit.com/api/me.json')
>>> me.json()['data']['has_mail']
True
```

Performing a simple search

We can use reddit's search API to search the entire site or in a subreddit. In this section we'll look at making a search API request. Proceed with the following steps to make a search request.

To make a search api call, we need to send a get request to `http://www.reddit.com/search.json` url with a search query `q` in the parameters.

```
>>> search = requests.get('http://www.reddit.com/search.json',
params={'q': 'python'})
>>> search.json().keys()
[u'kind', u'data']
>>> search.json()['data']['children'][0]['data'].keys()
```

```
[u'domain', u'author', u'media', u'score', u'approved_by', u'name',
u'created', u'url', u'author_flair_text', u'title' ... ]
```

The response to search is stored in the `search` variable which is a `requests.Response` object. The search results are stored in the `children` attribute of the `data` attribute. We can access `title`, `author`, `score` or another item in the search results as shown in the following example:

```
>>> search.json()['data']['children'][0]['data']['title']
u'If you could change something in Python what would it be?'
>>> search.json()['data']['children'][0]['data']['author']
u'yasoob_python'
>>> search.json()['data']['children'][0]['data']['score']
146
```

Searching subreddits

Searching in reddit's subreddits by title and description is same as searching in reddit. For that, we need to send a get request to `http://www.reddit.com/search.json` URL with a search query `q` in the parameters.

```
>>> subreddit_search = requests.get('http://www.reddit.com/subreddits/
search.json', params={'q': 'python'})
```

The response to search is stored in the `search` variable which is a `requests.Response` object. The search results are stored in the `data` attribute.

```
>>> subreddit_search.json()['data']['children'][0]['data']['title']
u'Python'
```

Summary

This chapter serves as a guide to interact with some of the most popular social media with Python using requests. We started by learning about the definition and importance of an API in the real world. Then we interacted with some of the most popular social networking sites like Twitter, Facebook and reddit. Each section about a social network will provide a hands on experience using a limited set of examples.

In the next chapter, we are going to learn step by step about Web scraping with requests and BeautifulSoup libraries.

Web Scraping with Python Requests and BeautifulSoup

6

We have become experts in how to communicate with the Web through `Requests`. Everything progressed flamboyantly while working with the APIs. However, there are some conditions where we need to be aware of API folklore.

The first thing that concerns us is not all web services have built an API for the sake of their third-party customers. Also, there is no statute that the API should be maintained perfectly. Even tech giants such as Google, Facebook, and Twitter tend to change their APIs abruptly without prior notice. So, it's better to understand that it is not always the API that comes to the rescue when we are looking for some vital information from a web resource.

The concept of **web scraping** stands as a savior when we really turn imperative to access some information from a web resource that does not maintain an API. In this chapter, we will discuss tricks of the trade to extract information from web resources by following all the principles of web scraping.

Before we begin, let's get to know some important concepts that will help us to reach our goal. Take a look at the response content format of a request, which will introduce us to a particular type of data:

```
>>> import requests
>>> r = requests.get("http://en.wikipedia.org/wiki/List_of_algorithms")
>>> r
<Response [200]>
>>> r.text
u'<!DOCTYPE html>\n<html lang="en" dir="ltr" class="client-nojs">\
n<head>\n<meta charset="UTF-8" />\n<title>List of algorithms - Wikipedia,
the free encyclopedia</title>\n...
```

In the preceding example, the response content is rendered in the form of semistructured data, which is represented using HTML tags; this in turn helps us to access the information about the different sections of a web page individually.

Now, let's get to know the different types of data that the Web generally deals with.

Types of data

In most cases, we deal with three types of data when working with web sources. They are as follows:

- Structured data
- Unstructured data
- Semistructured Data

Structured data

Structured data is a type of data that exists in an organized form. Normally, structured data has a predefined format and it is machine readable. Each piece of data that lies in structured data has a relation with every other data as a specific format is imposed on it. This makes it easier and faster to access different parts of data. The structured data type helps in mitigating redundant data while dealing with huge amounts of data.

Databases always contain structured data, and SQL techniques can be used to access data from them. We can regard census records as an example of structured data. They contain information about the date of birth, gender, place, income, and so on, of the people of a country.

Unstructured data

In contrast to structured data, unstructured data either misses out on a standard format or stays unorganized even though a specific format is imposed on it. Due to this reason, it becomes difficult to deal with different parts of the data. Also, it turns into a tedious task. To handle unstructured data, different techniques such as text analytics, Natural Language Processing (NLP), and data mining are used. Images, scientific data, text-heavy content (such as newspapers, health records, and so on), come under the unstructured data type.

Semistructured data

Semistructured data is a type of data that follows an irregular trend or has a structure which changes rapidly. This data can be a self described one, it uses tags and other markers to establish a semantic relationship among the elements of the data. Semistructured data may contain information that is transferred from different sources. **Scraping** is the technique that is used to extract information from this type of data. The information available on the Web is a perfect example of semistructured data.

What is web scraping?

In simple words, web scraping is the process of extracting desired data from a web resource. This method involves different procedures such as interacting with the web resource, choosing the appropriate data, obtaining information from the data, and converting the data to the desired format. With all the previous methods considered, a major spotlight will be thrown on the process of pulling the required data from the semistructured data.

Dos and don'ts of web scraping

Scraping a web resource is not always welcomed by the owners. Some companies put a restriction on using bots against them. It's etiquette to follow certain rules while scraping. The following are the dos and don'ts of web scraping:

- **Do refer to the terms and conditions**: The first thing that should come to our mind before we begin scraping is terms and conditions. Do visit the website's terms and conditions page and get to know whether they prohibit scraping from their site. If so, it's better to back off.

- **Don't bombard the server with a lot of requests**: Every website runs on a server that can serve only a specific amount of workload. It is equivalent to being rude if we bombard the server with lots of requests in a specific span of time, which may result in sever breakdown. Wait for some time between requests instead of bombarding the server with too many requests at once.

 Some sites put a restriction on the maximum number of requests processed per minute and will ban the request sender's IP address if this is not adhered to.

- **Do track the web resource from time to time**: A website doesn't always stay the same. According to its usability and the requirement of users, they tend to change from time to time. If any alteration has taken place in the website, our code to scrape may fail. Do remember to track the changes made to the site, modify the scrapper script, and scrape accordingly.

Predominant steps to perform web scraping

Generally, the process of web scraping requires the use of different tools and libraries such as the following:

- **Chrome DevTools or FireBug Add-on**: This can be used to pinpoint the pieces of information in an HTML/XML page.
- **HTTP libraries**: These can be used to interact with the server and to pull a response document. An example of this is `python-requests`.
- **Web scraping tools**: These are used to pull data from a semistructured document. Examples include `BeautifulSoup` or `Scrappy`.

The overall picture of web scraping can be observed in the following steps:

1. Identify the URL(s) of the web resource to perform the web scraping task.
2. Use your favorite HTTP client/library to pull the semistructured document.
3. Before extracting the desired data, discover the pieces of data that are in semistructured format.
4. Utilize a web scraping tool to parse the acquired semistructured document into a more structured one.
5. Draw the desired data that we are hoping to use. That's all, we are done!

Key web scraping tasks

While pulling the required data from a semistructured document, we perform various tasks. The following are the basic tasks that we adopt for scraping:

- **Searching a semistructured document:** Accessing a particular element or a specific type of element in a document can be accomplished using its `tag` name and `tag` attributes, such as `id`, `class`, and so on.
- **Navigating within a semistructured document**: We can navigate through a web document to pull different types of data in four ways, which are navigating down, navigating sideways, navigating up, and navigating back and forth. We can get to know more about these in detail later in this chapter.
- **Modifying a semistructured document:** By modifying the `tag` name or the `tag` attributes of a document, we can streamline and pull the required data.

What is BeautifulSoup?

The BeautifulSoup library is a simple yet powerful web scraping library. It has the capability to extract the desired data when provided with an HTML or XML document. It is charged with some superb methods, which help us to perform web scraping tasks effortlessly.

Document parsers

Document parsers aid us in parsing and serializing the semistructured documents that are written using HTML5, lxml, or any other markup language. By default, BeautifulSoup has Python's standard HTMLParser object. If we are dealing with different types of documents, such as HTML5 and lxml, we need to install them explicitly.

In this chapter, our prime focus will be laid only on particular parts of the library, which help us to understand the techniques to develop a practical scraping bot that we will build at the end of this chapter.

Installation

Installing BeautifulSoup is pretty straightforward. We can use pip to install it with ease:

```
$ pip install beautifulsoup4
```

Whenever we intend to scrape a web resource using BeautifulSoup, we need to create a BeautifulSoup object for it. The following are the commands to do this:

```
>>> from bs4 import BeautifulSoup
>>> soup = BeautifulSoup(<HTML_DOCUMENT_STRING>)
```

Objects in BeautifulSoup

The BeautifulSoup object parses the given HTML/XML document and converts it into a tree of Python objects, which are discussed in the following sections.

Tags

The word "tag" represents an HTML/XML tag in the provided document. Each tag object has a name and a lot of attributes and methods. The following example showcases the way to deal with a tag object:

```
>>> from bs4 import BeautifulSoup
>>> soup = BeautifulSoup("<h1 id='message'>Hello, Requests!</h1>")
```

In order to access the type, name, and attributes of the `BeautifulSoup` object, with `soup`, that we created in the preceding example, use the following commands:

- For accessing the `tag` type:

```
>>> tag = soup.h1
>>> type(tag)
<class 'bs4.element.Tag'>
```

- For accessing the `tag` name:

```
>>> tag.name
'h1'
```

- For accessing the `tag` attribute (`'id'` in the given html string)

```
>>> tag['id']
'message'
```

BeautifulSoup

The object that gets created when we intend to scrape a web resource is called a `BeautifulSoup` object. Put simply, it is the complete document that we are planning to scrape. This can be done using the following commands:

```
>>> from bs4 import BeautifulSoup
>>> soup = BeautifulSoup("<h1 id='message'>Hello, Requests!</h1>") >>>
type(soup)
<class 'bs4.BeautifulSoup'>
```

NavigableString

A `NavigableString` object represents the contents of `tag`. We use the `.string` attribute of the `tag` object to access it:

```
>>> tag.string
u'Hello, Requests!'
```

Comments

The `comment` object illustrates the comment part of the web document. The following lines of code exemplify a `comment` object:

```
>>> soup = BeautifulSoup("<p><!-- This is comment --></p>")
>>> comment = soup.p.string
>>> type(comment)
<class 'bs4.element.Comment'>
```

Web scraping tasks related to BeautifulSoup

As cited in the previous section of *Key web scraping tasks*, BeautifulSoup always follows those basic tasks in the process of web scraping. We can get to know these tasks in detail with the help of a practical example, using an HTML document. We will be using the following HTML document that is scraping_example.html, as an example through out the chapter:

```html
<!DOCTYPE html>
<html lang="en">
  <head>
    <meta charset="UTF-8" />
    <title>
      Chapter 6 - Web Scrapping with Python Requests and
      BeatuifulSoup
    </title>
  </head>
  <body>
    <div class="surveys">
      <div class="survey" id="1">
        <p class="question">
          <a href="/surveys/1">Are you from India?</a>
        </p>
        <ul class="responses">
          <li class="response">Yes - <span class="score">21</span>
          </li>
          <li class="response">No - <span class="score">19</span>
          </li>
        </ul>
      </div>
      <div class="survey" id="2">
        <p class="question">
          <a href="/surveys/2">Have you ever seen the rain?</a>
        </p>
        <ul class="responses">
          <li class="response">Yes - <span class="score">40</span>
          </li>
          <li class="response">No - <span class="score">0</span>
          </li>
        </ul>
      </div>
      <div class="survey" id="3">
        <p class="question">
          <a href="/surveys/1">Do you like grapes?</a>
        </p>
```

```
        <ul class="responses">
          <li class="response">Yes - <span class="score">34</span>
          </li>
          <li class="response">No - <span class="score">6</span>
          </li>
        </ul>
      </div>
    </div>
  </body>
</html>
```

To give a crystal clear understanding of the preceding web document, we showcased it as a document tree. The following diagram represents the preceding HTML document:

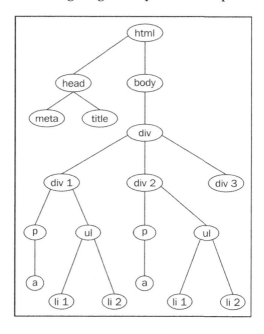

When we create the BeautifulSoup object for the previously shown web document, it will result in a tree of Python objects.

To perform different tasks with the previous document, scraping_example.html, we need to create a BeautifulSoup object. To create it, open the Python shell and run the following commands:

```
>>> from bs4 import BeautifulSoup
>>> soup = BeautifulSoup(open("scraping_example.html"))
```

From now, we will use the preceding `BeautifulSoup` object to execute different tasks. Let's perform the web scraping tasks on the `scraping_example.html` document and get an overall idea on all the tasks.

Searching the tree

To identify the different tags in an HTML/XML document, we need to search the whole document. In similar situations, we can use `BeautifulSoup` methods such as `find`, `find_all`, and so on.

Here is the syntax to search the whole document to identify the tags:

- `find(name, attributes, recursive, text, **kwargs)`
    - `name`: This is the first occurring tag name that appears in the process of discovery. It can be a string, a regular expression, a list, a function, or the value `True`.

- `find_all(name, attributes, recursive, text, limit, **kwargs)`
    - `name`: This is used to access specific types of tags with their name. It can be a string, a regular expression, a list, a function, or the value `True`.
    - `limit`: This is the maximum number of results in the output.

The common attributes for the preceding two methods are as follows:

- `attributes`: These are the attributes of an HTML/XML tag.
- `recursive`: This takes a Boolean value. If it is set to `True`, the `BeautifulSoup` library checks all the children of a specific tag. Vice versa, if it is set to `false`, the `BeautifulSoup` library checks the child at the next level only.
- `text`: This parameter identifies tags that consist of the string content.

Navigating within the tree

Different tasks are involved in navigating the document tree with the `Beautifulsoup4` module; they are discussed in the following section.

Navigating down

We can access a particular element's data by moving down in a document. If we consider the document tree in the previous figure, we can access different elements by moving downward from the top element—`html`.

Every element can be accessed using its `tag` name. Here is a way to access the contents of the `html` attribute:

```
>>> soup.html
<html lang="en">
...
...
</html>
```

Here are the ways in which we can access the elements of the preceding document tree by navigating down. In order to access the `title` element, we should go from top to bottom, that is, from `html` to `head` and from `head` to `title`, as shown in the following command:

```
>>> soup.html.head.title
<title>Chapter 6 - Web Scraping with Python Requests and BeatuifulSoup</title>
```

Similarly, you can access the `meta` element, as shown in the following command:

```
>>> soup.html.head.meta
<meta charset="utf-8"/>
```

Navigating sideways

To access the siblings in a document tree, we should navigate sideways. The `BeautifulSoup` library provides various `tag` object properties such as `.next_sibling`, `.previous_sibling`, `.next_siblings`, and `.previous_siblings`.

If you look at the preceding diagram containing the document tree, the different siblings at different levels of the tree, when navigated sideways, are as follows:

* `head` and `body`
* `div1`, `div2`, and `div3`

In the document tree, the `head` tag is the first child of `html`, and `body` is the next child of `html`. In order to access the children of the `html` tag, we can use its `children` property:

```
>>> for child in soup.html.children:
...     print child.name
...
head
body
```

To access the next sibling of `head` element we can use `.find_next_sibling`:

```
>>> soup.head.find_next_sibling()
<body>
    <div class="surveys">
        .
        .
        .
    </div>
</body>
```

To access the previous sibling of `body`, we can use `.find_previous_sibling`:

```
>>> soup.body.find_previous_sibling
<head><meta charset="utf-8"/><title>... </title></head>
```

Navigating up

We can access a particular element's parent by moving toward the top of the document tree. The `BeautifulSoup` library provides two properties— `.parent` and `.parents` — to access the first parent of the `tag` element and all its ancestors, respectively.

Here is an example:

```
>>> soup.div.parent.name
'body'


>>> for parent in soup.div.parents:
...       print parent.name
...
body
html
[document]
```

Navigating back and forth

To access the previously parsed element, we navigate back in the node of a tree, and to access the immediate element that gets parsed next, we navigate forward in the node of a tree. To deal with this, the `tag` object provides the `.find_previous_element` and `.find_next_element` properties, as shown in the following example:

```
>>> soup.head.find_previous().name
'html'
```

```
>>> soup.head.find_next().name
'meta'
```

Modifying the Tree

The BeautifulSoup library also facilitates us to make changes to the web document according to our requirements. We can alter a tag's properties using its attributes, such as the `.name`, `.string`, and `.append()` method. We can also add new tags and strings to an existing tag with the help of the `.new_string()` and `.new_tag()` methods. There are also other methods, such as `.insert()`, `.insert_before()`, `.insert_after()`, and so on, to make various modifications to the document tree.

Here is an example of changing the `title` tag's `.string` attribute:

- Before modifying the `title` tag the title contents are:

  ```
  >>> soup.title.string
  u'Chapter 6 - Web Scrapping with Python Requests and
  BeatuifulSoup'
  ```

- This is the way to modify the contents of a `title` tag:

  ```
  >>> soup.title.string = 'Web Scrapping with Python Requests and
  BeatuifulSoup by Balu and Rakhi'
  ```

- After the modifications the contents of the `tilte` tag looks like this:

  ```
  >>> soup.title.string
  u'Web Scrapping with Python Requests and BeatuifulSoup by Balu and
  Rakhi'
  ```

Building a web scraping bot – a practical example

At this point of time, our minds got enlightened with all sorts of clues to scrape the Web. With all the information acquired, let's look at a practical example. Now, we will create a web scraping bot, which will pull a list of words from a web resource and store them in a JSON file.

Let's turn on the scraping mode!

The web scraping bot

Here, the web scraping bot is an automated script that has the capability to extract words from a website named majortests.com. This website consists of various tests and **Graduate Record Examinations** (GRE) word lists. With this web scraping bot, we will scrape the previously mentioned website and create a list of GRE words and their meanings in a JSON file.

The following image is the sample page of the website that we are going to scrape:

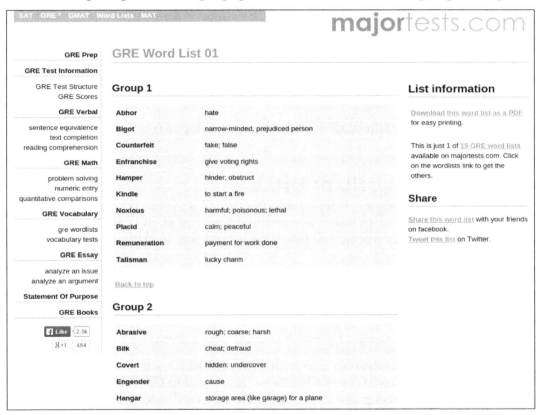

Before we kick start the scraping process, let's revise the dos and don't of web scraping as mentioned in the initial part of the chapter. Believe it or not they will definitely leave us in peace:

- **Do refer to the terms and conditions**: Yes, before scraping majortests.com, refer to the terms and conditions of the site and obtain the necessary legal permissions to scrape it.

- **Don't bombard the server with a lot of requests**: Keeping this in mind, for every request that we are going to send to the website, a delay has been instilled using Python's `time.sleep` function.

- **Do track the web resource from time to time**: We ensured that the code runs perfectly with the website that is running on the server. Do check the site once before starting to scrape, so that it won't break the code. This can be made possible by running some unit tests, which conform to the structure we expected.

Now, let's start the implementation by following the steps to scrape that we discussed previously.

Identifying the URL or URLs

The first step in web scraping is to identify the URL or a list of URLs that will result in the required resources. In this case, our intent is to find all the URLs that result in the expected list of GRE words. The following is the list of the URLs of the sites that we are going to scrape:

```
http://www.majortests.com/gre/wordlist_01,
```

```
http://www.majortests.com/gre/wordlist_02,
```

`http://www.majortests.com/gre/wordlist_03`, and so on

Our aim is to scrape words from nine such URLs, for which we found a common pattern. This will help us to crawl all of them. The common URL pattern for all those URLs is written using Python's `string` object, as follows:

```
http://www.majortests.com/gre/wordlist_0%d
```

In our implementation, we defined a method called `generate_urls`, which will generate the required list of URLs using the preceding URL string. The following snippet demonstrates the process in a Python shell:

```
>>> START_PAGE, END_PAGE = 1, 10
>>> URL = "http://www.majortests.com/gre/wordlist_0%d"
>>> def generate_urls(url, start_page, end_page):
...     urls = []
...     for page in range(start_page, end_page):
...         urls.append(url % page)
...     return urls
...
>>> generate_urls(URL, START_PAGE, END_PAGE)
['http://www.majortests.com/gre/wordlist_01', 'http://www.majortests.com/
gre/wordlist_02', 'http://www.majortests.com/gre/wordlist_03', 'http://
www.majortests.com/gre/wordlist_04', 'http://www.majortests.com/gre/
wordlist_05', 'http://www.majortests.com/gre/wordlist_06', 'http://
www.majortests.com/gre/wordlist_07', 'http://www.majortests.com/gre/
wordlist_08', 'http://www.majortests.com/gre/wordlist_09']
```

Using an HTTP client

We will use the `requests` module as an HTTP client to get the web resources:

```
>>> import requests
>>> def get_resource(url):
...     return requests.get(url)
...
>>> get_resource("http://www.majortests.com/gre/wordlist_01")
<Response [200]>
```

In the preceding code, the `get_resource` function takes `url` as an argument and uses the `requests` module to get the resource.

Discovering the pieces of data to scrape

Now, it is time to analyze and classify the contents of the web page. The content in this context is a list of words with their definitions. In order to identify the elements of the words and their definitions, we used Chrome DevTools. The perceived information of the elements (HTML elements) can help us to identify the word and its definition, which can be used in the process of scraping.

To carry this out open the URL (http://www.majortests.com/gre/wordlist_01) in the Chrome browser and access the **Inspect element** option by right-clicking on the web page:

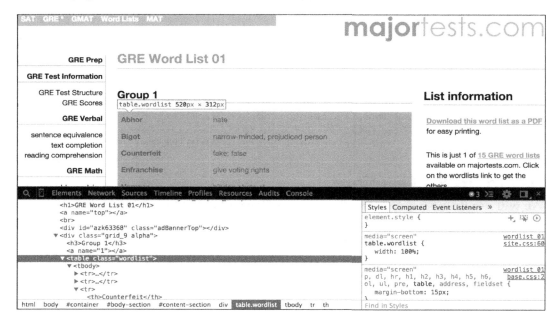

From the preceding image, we can identify the structure of the word list, which appears in the following manner:

```
<div class="grid_9 alpha">
  <h3>Group 1</h3>
  <a name="1"></a>
  <table class="wordlist">
    <tbody>
      <tr>
        <th>Abhor</th>
        <td>hate</td>
      </tr>
      <tr>
```

```
        <th>Bigot</th>
        <td>narrow-minded, prejudiced person</td>
      </tr>
      . . .
      . . .
    </tbody>
  </table>
</div>
```

By looking at the parts of the previously referred to web page, we can interpret the following:

- Each web page consists of a word list
- Every word list has many word groups that are defined in the same `div` tag
- All the words in a word group are described in a table having the class attribute — `wordlist`
- Each and every table row (`tr`) in the table represents a word and its definition using the `th` and `td` tags, respectively

Utilizing a web scraping tool

Let's use `BeautifulSoup4` as a web scraping tool to parse the obtained web page contents that we received using the `requests` module in one of the previous steps. By following the preceding interpretations, we can direct `BeautifulSoup` to access the required content of the web page and deliver it as an object:

```
def make_soup(html_string):
    return BeautifulSoup(html_string)
```

In the preceding lines of code, the `make_soup` method takes the `html` content in the form of a string and returns a `BeautifulSoup` object.

Drawing the desired data

The `BeautifulSoup` object that we obtained in the previous step is used to extract the required words and their definitions from it. Now, with the methods available in the `BeautifulSoup` object, we can navigate through the obtained HTML response, and then we can extract the list of words and their definitions:

```
def get_words_from_soup(soup):
    words = {}

    for count, wordlist_table in enumerate(
```

```
    soup.find_all(class_='wordlist')):

        title = "Group %d" % (count + 1)

        new_words = {}
        for word_entry in wordlist_table.find_all('tr'):
            new_words[word_entry.th.text] = word_entry.td.text

        words[title] = new_words

    return words
```

In the preceding lines of code, get_words_from_soup takes a BeautifulSoup object and then looks for all the words contained in the wordlists class using the instance's find_all() method, and then returns a dictionary of words.

The dictionary of words obtained previously will be saved in a JSON file using the following helper method:

```
def save_as_json(data, output_file):
    """ Writes the given data into the specified output file"""
    with open(output_file, 'w') as outfile:
        json.dump(data, outfile)
```

On the whole, the process can be depicted in the following program:

```
import json
import time

import requests

from bs4 import BeautifulSoup

START_PAGE, END_PAGE, OUTPUT_FILE = 1, 10, 'words.json'

# Identify the URL
URL = "http://www.majortests.com/gre/wordlist_0%d"


def generate_urls(url, start_page, end_page):
    """
    This method takes a 'url' and returns a generated list of url
strings

        params: a 'url', 'start_page' number and 'end_page' number
```

```
        return value: a list of generated url strings
    """
    urls = []
    for page in range(start_page, end_page):
        urls.append(url % page)
    return urls


def get_resource(url):
    """
    This method takes a 'url' and returns a 'requests.Response'
object

        params: a 'url'
        return value: a 'requests.Response' object
    """
    return requests.get(url)


def make_soup(html_string):
    """
    This method takes a 'html string' and returns a
'BeautifulSoup' object

        params: html page contents as a string
        return value: a 'BeautifulSoup' object
    """
    return BeautifulSoup(html_string)


def get_words_from_soup(soup):

    """
    This method extracts word groups from a given 'BeautifulSoup'
object

        params: a BeautifulSoup object to extract data
        return value: a dictionary of extracted word groups
    """

    words = {}
```

```python
        count = 0

        for wordlist_table in soup.find_all(class_='wordlist'):

            count += 1
            title = "Group %d" % count

            new_words = {}
            for word_entry in wordlist_table.find_all('tr'):
                new_words[word_entry.th.text] = word_entry.td.text

            words[title] = new_words
            print " - - Extracted words from %s" % title

        return words



def save_as_json(data, output_file):
    """ Writes the given data into the specified output file"""
            json.dump(data, open(output_file, 'w'))



def scrapper_bot(urls):
    """
    Scrapper bot:
        params: takes a list of urls

        return value: a dictionary of word lists containing
                        different word groups
    """

    gre_words = {}
    for url in urls:

        print "Scrapping %s" % url.split('/')[-1]

        # step 1

        # get a 'url'

        # step 2
```

```
        html = requets.get(url)

        # step 3
        # identify the desired pieces of data in the url using
Browser tools

        #step 4
        soup = make_soup(html.text)

        # step 5
        words = get_words_from_soup(soup)

        gre_words[url.split('/')[-1]] = words

        print "sleeping for 5 seconds now"
        time.sleep(5)

    return gre_words

if __name__ == '__main__':

    urls = generate_urls(URL, START_PAGE, END_PAGE+1)

    gre_words = scrapper_bot(urls)

    save_as_json(gre_words, OUTPUT_FILE)
```

Here is the content of the words.json file:

```
{"wordlist_04":
    {"Group 10":
        {"Devoured": "greedily eaten/consumed",
         "Magnate": "powerful businessman",
         "Cavalcade": "procession of vehicles",
         "Extradite": "deport from one country back to the home...
    .
    .
    .
}
```

Summary

In this chapter, you learned about different types of data that we encountered with web sources and tweaked some ideas. We came to know about the need for web scraping, the legal issues, and the goodies that it offers. Then, we jumped deep into web scraping tasks and their potential. You learned about a new library called `BeautifulSoup`, and its ins and outs, with examples.

We came to know the capabilities of `BeautifulSoup` in depth and worked on some examples to get a clear idea on it. At last, we created a practical scraping bot by applying the knowledge that we gained from the previous sections, which enlightened us with an experience to scrape a website in real time.

In the next chapter, you will learn about the Flask microframework and we will build an application using it by following the best practices.

7
Implementing a Web Application with Python Using Flask

To ensure prosperity in the process of learning about the Requests module, there seems to be nothing more important than an application of all the skills and knowledge that you attained until now. So, here we pave the way to apply the expertise you have gained till date, by creating a web application with the Flask framework. This will give you an in-depth knowledge of developing a practical web application and writing test cases for it. We do incline ourselves towards following the best practices and a hands-on approach in this process. Let us dive in to learn the stuff.

What is Flask?

Flask is a small yet powerful framework for creating web applications with Python. It can be called a **micro framework**. It is so small that if you could build a good rapport with it, you can understand all of its source code. It is powerful because of its goodies called **extensions** and its ability to provide all the basic services as a whole. The extensions can be added according to the application's requirement. The man behind Flask framework is Armin Ronacher, who released it on April 1, 2010.

Flask goodies are as follows:

- Flask comes up with an inbuilt development server, which assists you in the development process and in the testing of programs.

- Error logging is made simple in Flask, with its interactive web-based debugger. When executing your code, if any bug has emerged in the way, an error stack trace will be shown on the web page, which makes it easy to deal with. This can be achieved by setting the flag of app.debug to True.

- With its lightweight nature, Flask is a perfect framework to build RESTful web services. The route decorator which helps to bind a function to a URL can take the HTTP methods as arguments that pave a way to build API's in an ideal manner. In addition, working with JSON data is simple with Flask.

- The template support for Flask is served by a flexible template engine called **Jinja2**. This makes the process of rendering the templates a smoother task.

- The Session object is another goodie which saves the user's session. It stores the requests of the user so that the application can remember the different requests from the user.

- Flask uses the **Web Server Gateway Interface (WSGI)** protocol while dealing with requests from clients and it is 100 % WSGI compliant.

Getting started with Flask

We can kick-start our application development with a simple example, which gives you an idea of how we program in Python with a flask framework. In order to write this program, we need to perform the following steps:

1. Create a WSGI application instance, as every application in Flask needs one to handle requests from the client.

2. Define a route method which associates a URL and the function which handles it.

3. Activate the application's server.

Here is an example which follows the preceding steps to make a simple application:

```python
from flask import Flask
app = Flask(__name__)


@app.route("/")
```

```
def home():
    return "Hello Guest!"


if __name__ == "__main__":
    app.run()
```

In the preceding lines of code, we have created a WSGI application instance using the Flask's `Flask` class, and then we defined a route which maps the path "/" and the view function `home` to process the request using a Flask's decorator function `Flask.route()`. Next, we used the `app.run()` which tells the server to run the code. And at that end, it will result in a web page showing up `"Hello Guest!"`, when the code is executed.

Installing Flask

Before initiating the programming process, you will need to install the required dependencies. Let's initiate the installation process by creating a virtual environment using **virtual environment wrapper**. It's one of the best practices to use a virtual environment while creating an application. The virtual environment wrapper is a tool which puts all the dependencies of the project in one place.

This practice will mitigate a lot of complications while dealing with different projects in your system. In our tutorial the installation and application development goes forward using Python version 2.7.

The following are the steps for setting up the environment:

1. Install the virtual environment wrapper using `pip`. You may have to use `sudo` for administrative privileges:

   ```
   $ pip install virtualenvwrapper
   ```

2. All the installation packages related to virtual environments are placed in one folder for the sake of convenience. **Virtualenvwrapper** identifies the directory using an environmental variable WORKON_HOME. So, set the environmental variable to ~/Envs or anything of your choice.

   ```
   $ export WORKON_HOME=~/Envs
   ```

3. Create the WORKON_HOME directory using the following command if it doesn't exist on your local machine:

   ```
   $ mkdir -p $WORKON_HOME
   ```

4. In order to use the utilities provided by the `virtualenvwrapper`, we need to activate the shell script `virtualenvwrapper.sh` as shown in the following lines. On Ubuntu machines, we can find this script in the `/usr/local/bin` location:

```
$ source /usr/local/bin/virtualenvwrapper.sh
```

5. For the sake of convenience, add the commands in steps 2 and 4 to your shell startup file to initialize and activate the `virtualenvwrapper` utilities at your terminal's startup.

6. Now, use the `mkvirtualenv` command to create a new virtual environment for your project with the name `survey`. Once the `survey` environment is activated it gets displayed with the environment name in the closed braces before the shell prompt.

```
$ mkvirtualenv survey
New python executable in survey/bin/python
Installing setuptools, pip...done.
(survey) $
```

Installing required packages with pip

We are going to use **Flask-SQLAlchemy** in this project which is a Flask extension module that acts as an **Object Relational Mapper (ORM)** to interact with the database. We will also be using modules like `requests`, `httpretty`, `beautifulsoup` in the development of our `survey` application which we will be building in this tutorial.

Now install the following packages with your virtual environment activated:

```
(survey)~ $ pip install flask flask-sqlalchemy requests
httpretty beautifulsoup4
```

Survey – a simple voting application using Flask

To create the `survey` application, we are going to follow an approach which will give you an easy understanding of the ins and outs of the application and also will make this process of developing a joyride.

Our development procedure drives you through the process of getting you introduced to all the functions that the project deals with. And then, we will implement each and every function step-by-step. During the development process we will be following the **Model-View-Controller (MVC)** design pattern, which is popular for developing web applications.

The main aim of the `survey` application is to record the number of responses — `'yes'`, `'no'` and `'maybe'` - for the created survey questions.

Basic file structures

For developing a Flask application, we are following a specific structure to organize the contents of our application. Here is the file structure of the application that we are going to develop:

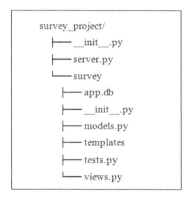

Here is a description of all the files and folders present in our application's file structure:

Name of the File/Folder	Description
`__init__.py`	Initializes our project and adds it to the `PYTHONPATH`
`server.py`	Invokes the application development server to startup.
`survey/__init__.py`	Initializes our application and brings various components into one place.
`survey/app.db`	A `sqlite3` file to store your data
`survey/models.py`	Defines the models of our application.
`survey/templates`	A place to put all the `Jinja2` templates.
`survey/tests.py`	A file in which various test cases related to the app are written.
`survey/views.py`	Defines the routes of your application.

In our Survey application, `survey_project` is the project root. Now, let us create all the files and folders with respect to the above file structure and place the following contents in the `survey_project/__init__.py` file.

```
import os
import sys
current_dir = os.path.abspath(os.path.dirname(os.path.dirname(__
file__)))
parent_dir = os.path.abspath(os.path.join(current_dir, os.pardir))
sys.path.insert(0, parent_dir)
```

Building the application

Now, we will introduce you to all the functions of the `survey` application. The following is the detailed set of tasks our application is bound to:

- Create survey questions
- View list of all questions
- View a specific question
- Modify a question
- Delete a question
- Up-vote a question

Every question stores information related to a specific survey. The fields that a `Question` model (a single definitive source of information about the data) contains are as follows:

- `id`: A primary key to identify each question uniquely
- `question_text`: Describes the survey
- `number_of_yes_votes`: Stores the number of `'yes'` votes polled
- `number_of_no_votes`: Stores the number of `'no'` votes polled
- `number_of_maybe_votes`: Stores the number of `'maybe'` votes polled

Now, let us start designing the resource holders, what we call URLs, for the previously mentioned tasks. These URLs need specific HTTP methods to communicate with the server.

The following table throws a spotlight on how we are going to design the URLs:

Task	HTTP method	URL
List of all questions	GET	`http://[hostname:port]/`
Create a survey question	POST	`http://[hostname:port]/questions`
View a specific question	GET	`http://[hostname:port]/questions/[question_id]`
Modify a question	PUT	`http://[hostname:port]/questions/[question_id]`
Delete a question	DELETE	`http://[hostname:port]/questions/[question_id]`
Up-vote a question	POST	`http://[hostname:port]/questions/[question_id]/vote`
Up-vote a question form	GET	`http://[hostname:port]/questions/[question_id]/vote`
New question form	GET	`http://[hostname:port]/questions/new`

Writing models with Flask-SQLAlchemy

SQLAlchemy is a Python Object Relational Mapper (ORM) and a query toolkit to interact with various databases. It provides a set of utilities which includes a base class to represent the models and a set of helper classes and functions to represent a database.

 A model is a logical representation of a table in a relational database which contains information about data.

Flask-SQLAlchemy is an extension to the Flask framework which adds support to SQLAlchemy.

Defining a model

While defining a model with Flask-SQLAlchemy, we need to keep the following three steps in mind:

1. Create a database instance.
2. Define a model using the database instance created before.
3. Call a method in the database instance to create the tables in the database.

Creating a database instance

In our application, we do need to create a database instance to store the data. For that, we need to configure the `'SQLALCHEMY_DATABASE_URI'` attribute in the WSGI application instance as shown in the following code. This code should be saved in the survey/__init__.py file.

__init__.py

```
import os

from flask import Flask
from flask.ext.sqlalchemy import SQLAlchemy

BASE_DIR = os.path.abspath(os.path.dirname(__file__))

app = Flask(__name__)
app.config['SQLALCHEMY_DATABASE_URI'] = \
    'sqlite:///' + os.path.join(BASE_DIR, 'app.db')
db = SQLAlchemy(app)
```

In the preceding lines of code, we created a WSGI application instance using the Flask's `Flask` class and configured the `'SQLALCHEMY_DATABASE_URI'` variable. Next, we created a database instance called db which is used to define models and to perform various queries.

Creating survey models

In order to store the data related to the survey application in the database, we should define a model called `Question`. This code lives in survey/models.py file.

models.py

```
class Question(db.Model):
    id = db.Column(db.Integer, primary_key=True)
    question_text = db.Column(db.String(200))
    number_of_yes_votes = db.Column(db.Integer, default=0)
    number_of_no_votes = db.Column(db.Integer, default=0)
    number_of_maybe_votes = db.Column(db.Integer, default=0)
```

In the preceding code, we defined the `Question` model which extends from db.Model. It contains five fields to store the data related to a specific survey:

* id
* question_text

- number_of_yes_votes
- number_of_no_votes
- number_of_maybe_votes

Now let us go ahead and add a constructor method, which enables us to set the instance variables for the Question object that we created in the previous lines of code:

```
class Question(db.Model):
    ...
    ...

    def __init__(self,
                 question_text,
                 number_of_yes_votes=0,
                 number_of_no_votes=0,
                 number_of_maybe_votes=0):

        self.question_text = question_text

        self.number_of_yes_votes = number_of_yes_votes
        self.number_of_maybe_votes = number_of_maybe_votes
        self.number_of_no_votes = number_of_no_votes
```

The preceding __init__() method takes the Question object and its values as parameters. Then, it will set the instance variables of the object that we passed.

Now, we will create a method called vote() which increments the counter variables for the 'yes', 'no' and 'maybe' votes.

```
class Question(db.Model):
    ...
    ...

    def vote(self, vote_type):
        if vote_type == 'yes':
            self.number_of_yes_votes += 1
        elif vote_type == 'no':
            self.number_of_no_votes += 1
        elif vote_type == 'maybe':
            self.number_of_maybe_votes += 1
        else:
            raise Exception("Invalid vote type")
```

In the preceding lines of code, we defined a `vote()` method, which takes the `Question` object as its first argument and the `vote_type` as its second argument. Based on the `vote_type` (`'yes'`, `'no'`, or `'maybe'`), the corresponding `number_of_<vote_type>_votes` of the `Question` object that we passed gets incremented.

Creating tables in the database

Now that we are done with defining the models related to our application using the database instance object called `db`, we need to create corresponding tables in the databases. For that, we need to call the method `create_all()`, which is present in the database instance — `db`.

In our application, we generally call this function before invoking the server defined in `runserver.py` file.

Querying database models

Now, we have the database models ready. Let us query the data from the database using the SQLAlchemy's ORM. We'll perform the basic create, retrieve, update, and delete (CRUD) operations on our database instance — `db`.

Before making queries, let us move to our project root directory and fire up the Python console to execute the following commands:

```
>>> from survey import app, db
>>> from survey.models import Question
```

Now, let us create a `Question` object in the database. Creating an object using SQLAlchemy's ORM involves three essential steps as shown in the following code:

```
>>> question = Question("Are you an American?")
>>> db.session.add(question)
>>> db.session.commit()
```

We can see that:

- The first step creates a Python object for the model.
- The next step adds the created Python object to the db's session.
- The last step involves committing the object to the database.

Retrieving the objects from the database is very simple using the ORM. The following query retrieves all the objects from the database:

```
>>> Question.query.all()
[<Question 1 - u'Are you an American?'>]
```

We can also retrieve a model object from the database using its primary key. If we look at the `Question` model, we have a primary key with the column name `id`. Now, let us go ahead and access it.

```
>>> Question.query.get(1)
<Question 1 - u'Are you an American?'>
```

It is time to vote a survey. Fetch the object with `id` value 1 and use its `vote()` method to increase the number of votes of that choice.

```
>>> question = Question.query.get(1)
>>> question.number_of_yes_votes
0
>>> question.vote('yes')
>>> db.session.add(question)
>>> db.session.commit()
```

Let us learn how to delete a record from the database using the `db.session.delete()` method as shown in the following code:

```
>>> question = Question.query.get(1)
>>> db.session.delete(question)
>>> db.session.commit()
```

If you try to access the same object, it will result in the `None` value.

```
>>> print Question.query.get(1)
None
```

Views

A view is a Python function, which receives a web request and sends back a web response. The response of a view can be a simple string, web page, the content of a file, or anything. Whenever a Flask application gets a request from the client, it will look for a `view` function to service it. The view contains the business logic which is necessary to process a request.

In the previous sections, we have created the necessary database models. Now, in this section, we will write the `view` functions. Let us create view for every resource we mentioned in the previous table, which throws spot light on how we are going to design the URLs. All the views should be created in the file `survey/views.py`.

List of all questions

This view shows all the surveys that we have created in the database. The Flask application will invoke this view whenever the client requests the root of the application. Add the following code to the `survey/views.py` file:

```
from flask import render_template
from survey import app
from survey.models import Question

@app.route('/', methods=['GET'])
def home():
    questions = Question.query.all()
    context = {'questions': questions,
               'number_of_questions': len(questions)}
    return render_template('index.html',
                           **context)
```

The `@app.route()` decorator maps the path `'/'` and the view function `home()`. The `home` view retrieves all the questions from the database using the SQLAlchemy ORM and renders a template named `'index.html'` using the `render_template` method. The `render_template` method takes the template name and a sequence of arguments to return a web page.

New survey

This view returns an HTML web form to create a new survey question. This view is called when a user visits the path `/questions/new`. Add the following code to the `survey/views.py` file:

```
.  .  .
.  .  .
@app.route('/questions/new', methods=['GET'])
def new_questions():
    return render_template('new.html')
```

Creating a new survey

This view creates a new survey in the database and shows the list of available questions as a response. This is invoked by the Flask application, when a user submits a request to a URL containing `/questions`, using the POST method. The data to create a new question can be accessed within a view using the `request.form` dictionary.

```
@app.route('/questions', methods=['POST'])
def create_questions():
```

```
        if request.form["question_text"].strip() != "":
            new_question = Question(question_text=request.form["question_
text"])
            db.session.add(new_question)
            db.session.commit()
            message = "Succefully added a new poll!"
        else:
            message = "Poll question should not be an empty string!"

        context = {'questions': Question.query.all(),
                   'message': message}
        return render_template('index.html',
                               **context)
```

Displaying a survey

This view shows the requested survey using the `question_id` argument passed in the URL. This view gets triggered when a user requests the path `'/questions/<question_id>'` with the HTTP `'GET'` verb:

```
@app.route('/questions/<int:question_id>', methods=['GET'])
def show_questions(question_id):
    context = {'question': Question.query.get(question_id)}
    return render_template('show.html',
                           **context)
```

Updating a survey

This view is used whenever a user wants to modify an existing question. This is invoked when a user submits the data to modify the `Question`. We can connect with this resource using HTTP's `'PUT'` method at `'/questions/<question_id>'`:

```
@app.route('/questions/<int:question_id>', methods=['PUT'])
def update_questions(question_id):
    question = Question.query.get(question_id)
    if request.form["question_text"].strip() != "":
        question.question_text = request.form["question_text"]
        db.session.add(question)
        db.session.commit()
        message = "Successfully updated a poll!"
    else:

        message = "Question cannot be empty!"

    context = {'question': question,
```

```
                                       'message': message}

        return render_template('show.html',
                               **context)
```

Deleting a survey

This view is used to delete a specific survey from the database. The specific survey is identified based on the `question_id` value passed in the URL. The users can access this web page at `'/questions/<question_id>'` using the `'DELETE'` HTTP verb. Once the question gets deleted from the database, the user will be prompted with a message and a list of available questions.

```
@app.route('/questions/<int:question_id>', methods=['DELETE'])
def delete_questions(question_id):
    question = Question.query.get(question_id)
    db.session.delete(question)
    db.session.commit()
    context = {'questions': Question.query.all(),
               'message': 'Successfully deleted'}
    return render_template('index.html',
                           **context)
```

New vote form to caste a vote in a survey

This view returns a web page containing a HTML form to vote a particular choice in a survey. It can be accessed at `'/questions/<question_id>/vote'`.

```
@app.route('/questions/<int:question_id>/vote', methods=['GET'])
def new_vote_questions(question_id):
    question = Question.query.get(question_id)
    context = {'question': question}
    return render_template('vote.html',
                           **context)
```

Casting a vote to a particular choice in a survey

This view is used to cast a new vote to a particular choice in a survey. The user has to submit the specific choice to the resource `'/questions/<question_id>/vote'` using the `'POST'` method. After the successful casting of a vote, the user is redirected to the survey details page.

```
@app.route('/questions/<int:question_id>/vote', methods=['POST'])
```

```
def create_vote_questions(question_id):
    question = Question.query.get(question_id)

    if request.form["vote"] in ["yes", "no", "maybe"]:
        question.vote(request.form["vote"])

    db.session.add(question)
    db.session.commit()
    return redirect("/questions/%d" % question.id)
```

Templates

A template is a simple text document which contains block tags or variables. **Flask micro-framework** makes use of the `Jinja2` template engine for rendering the HTML pages.

In our application, we use five different templates which includes a `base` template — `base.html`. This `base` template is a layout consisting of the common elements of all the templates. The four other templates (`index.html`, `show.html`, `vote.html` and `new.html`) make use of a concept called **template inheritance** provided by the `Jinja2` template engine. It is used to enable those common features to get showed up without a redundant code in every template.

The base template

This template is a skeleton for all the other templates. It contains a common navigation menu section and a placeholder to hold the primary content block of every page in this application. The `survey/templates/base.html` template will contain the following code:

```
<html>
  <head>
    <title>Welcome to Survey Application</title>
  </head>
  <body>
    {% if message %}
        <p style="text-align: center;">{{ message }}</p>
    {% endif %}
    <div>
      <a href="/">Home</a> |
      <a href="/questions">All Questions</a> |
      <a href="/questions/new">Create a new Question</a>
    </div>
```

```
    <hr>
    {% block content %}{% endblock %}
  </body>
</html>
```

The list of questions template

As we need to show the list of questions in a web page, we iterate over the questions variable using a for loop tag and display all the vote counts of a specific survey. Add the following to the survey/templates/index.html file:

```
{% extends "base.html" %}

{% block content %}
    <p>Number of Questions - <span id="number_of_questions">{{
number_of_questions }}</span></p>
    {% for question in questions %}
    <div>
        <p>
            <p><a href="/questions/{{ question.id }}">{{
question.question_text }}</a></p>
            <ul>
                <li>Yes - {{ question.number_of_yes_votes }} </li>
                <li>No - {{ question.number_of_no_votes }} </li>
                <li>Maybe - {{ question.number_of_maybe_votes }}
</li>
            </ul>
        </p>
    </div>
    {% endfor %}
    <hr />
{% endblock %}
```

Creating a new survey template

To show an HTML form containing a new survey question, we defined a template called survey/templates/new.html:

new.html

```
{% extends "base.html" %}

{% block content %}
    <h1>Create a new Survey</h1>
    <form method="POST" action="/questions">
```

```
        <p>Question: <input type="text" name="question_text"></p>
        <p><input type="submit" value="Create a new Survey"></p>
    </form>
{% endblock %}
```

Showing the details of a survey template

To display all the details of a survey, create a template in the following way. This template also includes a link to the cast your vote page. Add the following code to the survey/templates/show.html file:

```
{% extends "base.html" %}

{% block content %}
    <div>
        <p>
        {% if question %}
            <p>{{ question.question_text }}</p>
            <ul>
                <li>Yes - {{ question.number_of_yes_votes }}</li>
                <li>No - {{ question.number_of_no_votes }}
</li>
                <li>Maybe - {{
question.number_of_maybe_votes}}</li>
            </ul>
            <p><a href="/questions/{{ question.id }}/vote">Cast
your vote now</a></p>
        {% else %}
            Not match found!
        {% endif %}
        </p>
    </div>
    <hr />
{% endblock %}
```

Casting a vote template

To cast a vote, we need to display a web page containing a HTML form with a survey and its choices. Add the following code to the survey/templates/vote.html file:

```
{% extends "base.html" %}

{% block content %}
    <div>
```

```
    <p>
    {% if question %}
        <p>{{ question.question_text }}</p>

        <form action="/questions/{{ question.id }}/vote"
method="POST">
            <input type="radio" name="vote"
value="yes">Yes<br>
            <input type="radio" name="vote" value="no">No<br>
            <input type="radio" name="vote"
value="maybe">Maybe<br>

            <input type="submit" value="Submit" /><br>
        </form>
        <p><a href="/questions/{{ question.id }}">Back to
Question</a></p>
    {% else %}
        Not match found!
    {% endif %}
    </p>
    </div>
    <hr />
{% endblock %}
```

Running the survey application

Hurray! We succeeded in creating an application which will allow the users to create a survey, retrieve a survey, update a survey, delete a survey, and cast the vote of a choice for a survey. Perform the following steps for running the server:

1. Before running the server, let us go ahead and fill the contents of `server.py` with the following code:

```
import sys

from survey import app, db
from survey import views

def main():
    db.create_all()
    app.run(debug=True)
    return 0

if __name__ == '__main__':
    sys.exit(main())
```

2. Now, let us run the application using the `runserver.py` script as shown in the following lines:

```
$ python runserver.py
* Running on http://127.0.0.1:5000/
* Restarting with reloader
```

3. Now, the server is up and running. To access the application on a web browser, visit the URL—`http://127.0.0.1:5000/`.

We are done!

Writing unit tests to survey applications

Creating an application without test cases is half done. Even though you take a lot of care while developing the application, there might be a chance of encountering errors at some point. Writing test cases will always leave us at a safe point.

In this section, we are going to write unit test cases for some tasks in our survey application. Add the following test case code to `survey/tests.py` file:

```python
import unittest
import requests

from bs4 import BeautifulSoup
from survey import db
from survey.models import Question

class TestSurveyApp(unittest.TestCase):

    def setUp(self):
        db.drop_all()
        db.create_all()

    def test_defaults(self):
        question = Question('Are you from India?')
        db.session.add(question)
        db.session.commit()

        self.assertEqual(question.number_of_yes_votes, 0)
        self.assertEqual(question.number_of_no_votes, 0)
        self.assertEqual(question.number_of_maybe_votes, 0)

    def test_votes(self):
        question = Question('Are you from India?')
```

```
        question.vote('yes')
        db.session.add(question)
        db.session.commit()

        self.assertEqual(question.number_of_yes_votes, 1)
        self.assertEqual(question.number_of_no_votes, 0)
        self.assertEqual(question.number_of_maybe_votes, 0)

    def test_title(self):
        title = "Welcome to Survey Application"
        response = requests.get("http://127.0.0.1:5000/")
        soup = BeautifulSoup(response.text)
        self.assertEqual(soup.title.get_text(),
                         title)
```

We can see the following from the preceding block of code:

- The initial lines of code import all the necessary modules into the memory.

- The setUp() method in the TestSurveyApp drops all the existing tables and creates them for every test case.

- The test_defaults test case will test the defaults of the Question object that was created. If the defaults do not match the expected inputs, the test case fails.

- The test_votes() will up-vote a specific choice for a survey and test whether the voted choice gets incremented and other choices remain the same.

- The test_title() will test whether the title of a response matches with the expected title. It uses the BeautifulSoup library to access the title from the response contents.

Summary

In this chapter, we learnt about the Flask micro-framework and looked at the different features of Flask. We also set up a virtual environment using virtualenvwrapper, and created a web application using Flask, Flask-SQLAlchemy, and Jinja2. Finally, we wrote unit tests for the developed application.

Index

Thank you for buying
Python Requests Essentials

About Packt Publishing

Packt, pronounced 'packed', published its first book, *Mastering phpMyAdmin for Effective MySQL Management*, in April 2004, and subsequently continued to specialize in publishing highly focused books on specific technologies and solutions.

Our books and publications share the experiences of your fellow IT professionals in adapting and customizing today's systems, applications, and frameworks. Our solution-based books give you the knowledge and power to customize the software and technologies you're using to get the job done. Packt books are more specific and less general than the IT books you have seen in the past. Our unique business model allows us to bring you more focused information, giving you more of what you need to know, and less of what you don't.

Packt is a modern yet unique publishing company that focuses on producing quality, cutting-edge books for communities of developers, administrators, and newbies alike. For more information, please visit our website at www.packtpub.com.

About Packt Open Source

In 2010, Packt launched two new brands, Packt Open Source and Packt Enterprise, in order to continue its focus on specialization. This book is part of the Packt Open Source brand, home to books published on software built around open source licenses, and offering information to anybody from advanced developers to budding web designers. The Open Source brand also runs Packt's Open Source Royalty Scheme, by which Packt gives a royalty to each open source project about whose software a book is sold.

Writing for Packt

We welcome all inquiries from people who are interested in authoring. Book proposals should be sent to author@packtpub.com. If your book idea is still at an early stage and you would like to discuss it first before writing a formal book proposal, then please contact us; one of our commissioning editors will get in touch with you.

We're not just looking for published authors; if you have strong technical skills but no writing experience, our experienced editors can help you develop a writing career, or simply get some additional reward for your expertise.

Python Network Programming Cookbook

ISBN: 978-1-84951-346-3   Paperback: 234 pages

Over 70 detailed recipes to develop practical solutions for a wide range of real-world network programming tasks

1. Demonstrates how to write various besopke client/server networking applications using standard and popular third-party Python libraries.

2. Learn how to develop client programs for networking protocols such as HTTP/HTTPS, SMTP, POP3, FTP, CGI, XML-RPC, SOAP and REST.

3. Provides practical, hands-on recipes combined with short and concise explanations on code snippets.

IPython Notebook Essentials

ISBN: 978-1-78398-834-1   Paperback: 190 pages

Compute scientific data and execute code interactively with NumPy and SciPy

1. Perform Computational Analysis interactively.

2. Create quality displays using matplotlib and Python Data Analysis.

3. Step-by-step guide with a rich set of examples and a thorough presentation of The IPython Notebook.

Please check **www.PacktPub.com** for information on our titles

Python Data Analysis

ISBN: 978-1-78355-335-8   Paperback: 348 pages

Learn how to apply powerful data analysis techniques with popular open source Python modules

1. Learn how to find, manipulate, and analyze data using Python.

2. Perform advanced, high performance linear algebra and mathematical calculations with clean and efficient Python code.

3. An easy-to-follow guide with realistic examples that are frequently used in real-world data analysis projects.

Python for Secret Agents

ISBN: 978-1-78398-042-0   Paperback: 216 pages

Analyze, encrypt, and uncover intelligence data using Python, the essential tool for all aspiring secret agents

1. Build a toolbox of Python gadgets for password recovery, currency conversion, and civic data hacking.

2. Use stenography to hide secret messages in images.

3. Get to grips with geocoding to find villains' secret lairs.

Please check **www.PacktPub.com** for information on our titles

Made in the USA
Las Vegas, NV
03 June 2021